OPPORTUNITIES IN
WELDING CAREERS

Mark Rowh

Foreword by
Richard M. Alley
President
American Welding Society

VGM Career Horizons
a division of *NTC Publishing Group*
Lincolnwood, Illinois USA

Cover Photo Credits:
Front cover: upper left and lower
left, Mountain View College photos;
upper right, American Welding
Society photo; lower right, Bessemer
State Technical College photo.
Back cover: upper left, American
Welding Society photo; upper right,
Bessemer State Technical College
photo; lower left, Lincoln Electric
Company photo; lower right, Mountain
View College photo.

Library of Congress Cataloging-in-Publication Data

Rowh, Mark.
  Opportunities in welding careers / Mark Rowh ; foreword by Richard M. Alley.

      p.   cm. — (VGM opportunities series)
      ISBN 0-8442-8598-6 : $12.95. — ISBN 0-8442-8599-4 (pbk.) : $9.95
      1. Welding—Vocational guidance.   I. Title.   II. Series.
TS227.7.R68   1990
671.5'2'023—dc20   90-31085
                                                                         CIP

Published by VGM Career Horizons, a division of NTC Publishing Group.
© 1990 by NTC Publishing Group, 4255 West Touhy Avenue,
Lincolnwood (Chicago), Illinois 60646-1975 U.S.A.

0 1 2 3 4 5 6 7 8 9 VP 9 8 7 6 5 4 3 2 1

ABOUT THE AUTHOR

Mark Rowh is a widely published writer as well as an experienced educator in community college and vocational-technical education. A member of the administrative staff at New River Community College in Dublin, Virginia, he has also held administrative positions at Greenville Technical College in South Carolina and Bluefield State College and Parkersburg Community College in West Virginia.

In his educational career, Rowh has worked closely with a variety of technical programs. He also holds a doctorate in vocational and technical education from Clemson University.

Rowh's articles on educational and management topics have appeared in more than fifty magazines. He previously contributed *Opportunities in Drafting Careers* to the VGM Opportunities series and is the author of *Coping with Stress in College,* published by College Board Books.

ACKNOWLEDGMENTS

The author greatly appreciates the cooperation of the following in researching and writing this book:

American Welding Society
Greenville Technical College
International Association of Machinists and Aerospace Workers
National Association of Trade and Technical Schools

FOREWORD

From production in leading-edge industries to pioneering research in world-class university laboratories, careers in welding offer a wide variety of career opportunities. Yet, as we approach the year 2000, shortages of young people entering the welding industry persist at all levels. At production levels, the welding industry is getting only one replacement for every four who leave due to retirement or job change. From welding engineers to researchers seeking to unlock the secrets of the welding arc, comparable shortfalls are reported. The welding industry is full of opportunity.

The fact is that welding is involved in producing more than 50 percent of the gross national product in manufacturing. And as robots enter the industry, the influx of computers and space-age new materials is making the welding industry a most exciting and challenging environment.

New excitement also is coming into the welding industry as new welding and joining processes are developed, as the industry rapidly globalizes, and as a new certification program for welders is being introduced by the American Welding Society.

Upward mobility in the industry is unusually great. You may enter with a high school education and advance as you gain experience and continue your education. The industry, including the American Welding Society, is stepping up its support of education with new, increased scholarship and research grants.

Mobility also is abundant if you later choose to move into sales, application engineering, safety, design, or research. And experienced welders have the option of training and testing to become certified welding inspectors.

Opportunities in welding careers are varied, affording you wide choices to build on your experience and education as you mature and your career goals may change.

Richard M. Alley
President
American Welding Society
1989–1990

INTRODUCTION

Any decision regarding career choices is not to be taken lightly. Such choices need to be made with as much information available to support them as possible.

Every career field has its own advantages and disadvantages, and welding is no different. The advantages can be significant, however, for persons with the right interests and aptitudes. This book describes an occupation that many men and women find both challenging and genuinely important. As with many other technical fields, the work performed by welders is key to many industries and manufacturing efforts. At the same time, welders enjoy a wide range of work settings and job tasks.

For any reader interested in considering a welding career, this book is offered as an overview of the basic facts one needs to render a well-informed decision. It is hoped that the material provided here accurately conveys the relevant details needed for a basic understanding of this fascinating career field.

DEDICATION

This book is dedicated to the memory of Roland Wobbe, whose kind and thoughtful encouragement provided much of the impetus to my writing career.

CONTENTS

What welding is. History of welding. Modern welding. Advantages of a welding career. Looking at a welding career in greater detail.

Major welding processes. New types of welding. Related technologies. The diversity of welding processes.

Where welders work. Other work environments. Job titles. Tools, supplies, and equipment used in welding. A day in the life of a welder. Welding safely. Questions to ask yourself.

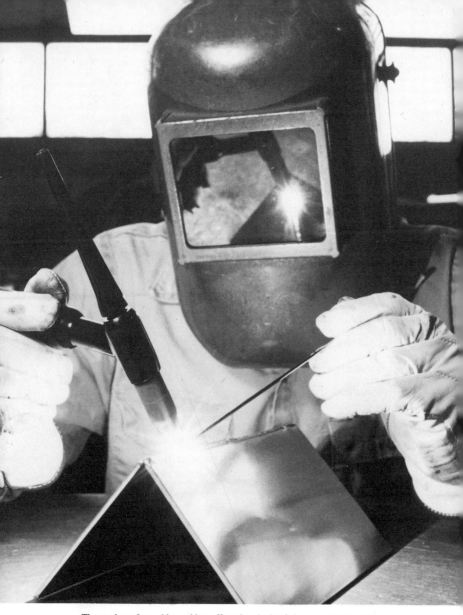

The work performed by welders affects hundreds of elements of daily life.
(American Welding Society photo)

CHAPTER 1

THE IMPORTANCE OF WELDING

Welding is one of the most vital processes of modern civilization. Such importance may not be so apparent at first glance, but all around us the work of welders holds a key place in our lives.

Consider, for example, a trip to the nearest mall. Whether you take a car or bus, the machine that transports you has been assembled at least in part by welding. Along the path of your journey, you will cross bridges constructed with the assistance of welders. Once you arrive at the mall, the beautiful buildings accommodating hundreds of shoppers stand as monuments to the work of welders and other craftspersons. And many of the products sold within the various retail stores could not have been assembled without welding. From the framework of bicycles or exercise cycles to washing machines, dryers, and other appliances, welded materials abound.

In the same way, the work performed by welders affects hundreds of other elements of daily life. The electrical power that energizes homes, schools, and factories emanates from power plants constructed in part by welders. Commercial airliners, tractor-trailer rigs, office buildings, guided missiles, and more owe a similar debt to the welding field. The list could go on and on, but the bottom line is that welding plays an extremely important part in many areas of life.

WHAT WELDING IS

Exactly what is welding? There are different types of welding, but they all share a common definition: welding is the joining of two or more materials through heat, pressure, or a related process. The application of the welding process causes the materials to fuse together, forming in essence a single piece of material where two or more previously existed.

Welding may be involved in the construction of equipment, moving vehicles, buildings, or other items both large and small. Or it may consist of repairs or modifications to existing devices. In either case, the work requires special knowledge and equipment. The need for personnel who have this special knowledge means that individuals trained in welding continue to encounter a significant level of job demand. Welders not only have contributed in a major way to past developments but can be expected to continue their essential work for decades to come.

HISTORY OF WELDING

The first modern welding processes were invented about a hundred years ago. But long before that time, various techniques for working with metal had been developed. In fact, much of history has been defined by humans' capabilities for working with metal and other materials.

Primitive Metalworking

First there was the Stone Age, when men and women first began to use technology. Of course this was very primitive, consisting largely of striking one rock against another in making stone scrapers, knives, and simple weapons. For hundreds of thousands of years, the use of metal was an unimagined possibility waiting to be discovered.

Then someone discovered copper, one of the softest and most easily worked metals, and figured out how to shape it into jewelry, cooking utensils, and other devices. Two other soft metals, gold and silver, were also found to be easily worked into various forms for jewelry and other items.

Although these metals were useful for some applications, they were too soft to be effective for many uses. A sword made of copper or gold, for example, would not be hard enough to stand up against weapons made of stone or other materials.

Discovery of Alloys

A partial answer was developed with the discovery of alloys. By combining two or more metals, men found that they could create a new metal with different characteristics from the original materials. The most important of these was bronze, an alloy of copper and tin. Early metal workers fashioned bronze into knives, swords, shields, eating utensils, and many other items. This metal made such a profound impact on civilization, in fact, that historians have used the name Bronze Age to designate the period of history when its use became common.

Discovery of Iron and Steel

Even more important was the discovery of iron and, later, steel. When men first learned to smelt iron ore and obtain what was at that point the toughest metal ever known, they initiated a new era in human technology. Warriors equipped with weapons made of iron or steel found they had a tremendous advantage over opponents who were not, and empires formed and flourished thanks in great part to this new metal. Iron and steel were used not just in weapons but also in everyday items such as axes, knives, and other tools.

Over the centuries, the use of iron and steel became increasingly common. Medieval knights protected themselves in armor made of steel, and later, the Industrial Revolution saw an explosion of inventions, many of which depended on the use of iron, steel, and other metals. One of the most important was the railroad, which fostered the use of great quantities of metal in tracks as well as trains themselves.

Early Welding

The first instances of actual welding occurred in the 1880s. Both in Europe and the United States, pioneers in the field developed and refined techniques for fusion welding and several related processes. Once the concept of welding had been proven workable, researchers and practicing welders continued developing new and innovative processes, leading eventually to the diversity of today's multifaceted welding field. Many of these developments came along during the early part of the twentieth century as initiatives in other technologies were adapted for use in welding.

As with many other technical developments, the needs of warfare acted as a catalyst for improvement of welding technology, particularly in the areas of mass production. The need to produce thousands of tanks, planes, ships, and other vehicles during World War II, for example, expanded the parameters of the welding profession. The same was true of postwar economic growth in the automobile industry, construction industry, and other areas of civilian as well as military life.

MODERN WELDING

New Methods

Modern welding incorporates many of the principles developed earlier this century along with the latest in technological advancements. Since World War II, advances in welding have mirrored other developments in technology. The invention of the laser, for example, led to the creation of laser beam welding as an option to traditional welding methodology. Advances in various aspects of automated manufacturing have contributed to improvements in welding machines designed to perform assembly-line work and other increasingly automated tasks. The growing use of new kinds of plastics has precipitated the development of techniques for welding plastics. General advances in physics and electronics have contributed to varied welding applications such as electron beam welding and the use of ultrasonic welding machines.

Thanks to scores of scientific and technological breakthroughs, welding continues to be a field where new techniques add to traditional capabilities. The result is a field where existing workers do not tend to find themselves being bypassed by advancing technology, but instead realize enhancements in their work that make the field more diverse than ever before.

New Applications

Not only have new methods of welding emerged in recent years, but many new applications for welding have come about. The space program, for example, depends on the work of welders in constructing rocket boosters, launch structures, and other related equipment. The creation of military and civilian aircraft has likewise become increasingly sophisticated. The construction of nuclear power plants is another area where practices perfected over the last few decades are being applied to what might be considered a futuristic task. In virtually all sectors of modern civilization, welders play some kind of role, whether that means constructing habitats for working and living or building and repairing important equipment.

Welding Techniques

Today's welder can choose from among a variety of techniques. He or she might utilize the relatively simple technology involved in gas welding, where a special torch is used to burn a gas such as acetylene, producing a flame that is hot enough to melt metal. In this process, the welder usually holds the torch and completes the work by hand.

Welders also carry out arc welding, where instead of creating heat through combustion of gases, high temperatures are achieved through an electric arc. Here, the welder generally uses a generator to produce electric current and a welding rod or electrode to create the necessary electric arc.

A number of different methodologies can be used to practice arc welding.

Another technique is known as resistance welding. Instead of an arc, electricity is controlled to create resistance as it flows between pieces of metal, fusing them together.

Still other types of welding take advantage of recent developments in other fields. Some of these modern techniques are based on such advanced technologies as lasers, electron beams, and waves of ultrasound.

More details about the major welding processes are provided in chapter 2. The main point to remember here, though, is that welding is truly a diverse field. The act of welding might involve the manual use of a welding torch and portable gas tanks. Or it might mean the operation of a complicated automated welding machine. Being employed as a welder can mean working for an automobile factory, the government, a large construction company, or a small welding shop. The person who becomes a welder might take a job in his or her home town or might end up helping construct an electric plant in Saudi Arabia or an oil rig in the North Sea. With so many options, a career in welding can certainly meet a wide range of possibilities.

ADVANTAGES OF A WELDING CAREER

Persons who pursue a career in welding choose this field for a variety of reasons. Among them are the following advantages.

The Satisfaction of Performing Skilled Work

If you have ever held a part-time job or other employment, you know that working has its good and bad points. Every job features both ups and downs, but not every kind of work provides satisfaction in accomplishing the tasks at hand. This is especially true for many jobs that require no special skills or training. For instance, many workers find difficulty in deriving satisfaction from such jobs as collecting garbage, standing and holding signs for a highway construction crew, or cleaning motel rooms. This is not to say there is anything wrong with such positions or the people who hold them, but it is not unusual to find that those working in such jobs obtain little pleasure from performing them.

A job such as welding, on the other hand, often provides a more satisfying work experience. After all, welders perform detailed work that a person who has not had the right training simply cannot do. The fact that special skills are needed helps boost a sense of accomplishment in work that requires skill, patience, and diligence.

Too, there is something inherently satisfying in building something. Working in cooperation with other craftspersons, welders help construct some of the largest and most advanced structures known to the world. Can you imagine watching the christening of a huge aircraft carrier or merchant ship and realizing that you helped construct it? Or on a less grandiose scale, how do you think it would feel to do a good job of building or repairing a small appliance? In either case, the satisfaction of building something useful or making a key repair to an item of value can provide a genuine measure of satisfaction.

The Right Type of Work Setting

A popular rock song from the 1970s touts the philosophy of "different strokes for different folks," referring to the old truism that people have different likes and dislikes. This is as true in the area of careers as in anything else. Some people love to sit at a desk and manipulate words or figures all day, for instance, while to others, such a job would be tremendously boring. Some people prefer to work indoors; others enjoy putting in their hours outside whenever possible. Still others like to supervise people more than any other function.

Depending on your own preferences, a career in welding may provide just the right environment. If working in an office does not sound appealing, the basic hands-on approach involved in welding might be more suitable. Of course job environments vary according to the type of welding being performed, but the range of possibilities can include working outdoors, on the floor of a factory, or in a small shop setting. In fact, some welders (such as those in building construction) move frequently from one job site to the next, encountering many different job environments.

If your idea of the right job involves wearing a three-piece suit or fancy dress to work every day and making your living from behind a desk, then a welding career probably does not represent a smart choice. If, on the other hand, you enjoy working with equipment and have a flair for building things, this field may be ideal. A welding career can allow you the chance to work in a setting where you feel unfettered by office politics, the need to maintain an expensive wardrobe, or other restrictions found in many careers.

Good Pay and Benefits

Welders earn good pay, and that is a major point of attraction for many workers. As discussed more fully in later chapters, welders earn higher-than-average wages around the country. Persons willing to invest a modest amount of time in a welding training program almost always find their efforts pay off many times over. Welding not only offers more money than most unskilled jobs but also more than many jobs where collegiate study or other special preparation is needed.

Most welding jobs also include a variety of fringe benefits such as medical insurance, retirement plans, and other important support. In many instances, such benefits are provided through a union contract, where a labor union has worked intensively to gain the best possible package of wages and benefits for its members. Even in nonunion environments, however, welders usually earn good benefits along with attractive wages.

A Field That Should Not Become Outdated

With the rapid changes in contemporary life, a major consideration in any career decision should be its potential for the future. Too often, careers that sound promising today become obsolete suddenly when some new technology explodes on the scene.

Of course no guarantees can be issued for any field, but experts in welding feel a need for this process will continue on a long-term basis. Technological advancements may change the way in which many welding processes are conducted, but welding itself will continue to be important. Tomorrow's welders may be constructing components for a space station or a new type of ocean-going vehicle, among other things, but they will still be welding a variety of metals and other materials. For many years to come, men and women skilled in applying welding techniques are projected to be needed in a variety of manufacturing fields and other areas.

In its brochure "Welding and Joining," the American Welding Society lists these advantages of a welding career:

- Job opportunities immediately after high school (with vocational-technical studies)
- Opportunities for growth through new and emerging technologies
- A variety of jobs and duties
- Job security based on a skill needed for national production

- Competitive wages
- Opportunities for jobs in a variety of locations

LOOKING AT A WELDING CAREER
IN GREATER DETAIL

The remainder of this book provides an overview of various factors involved in a career in welding. Chapter 2 looks at the major welding processes. Chapter 3 covers typical jobs performed by welders and the variety in working environments. In chapter 4, you will find an overview of the educational process needed to prepare for a welding career along with tips for negotiating the educational process. Chapter 5 discusses special programs where training can be obtained, while chapter 6 covers organizations and certifications. Earnings and benefits are covered in chapter 7. The range of opportunities in the field is noted in chapter 8, and tips on getting started in welding are covered in chapter 9.

In addition, two helpful appendices are included to provide you with additional information for possible use in considering or planning for a welding career. All told, the book provides a detailed look at welding careers and how you might fit in. Read on, and you may find that a welding career offers something for you.

Gas metal arc welding (GMAW) is one of the most common welding processes. (Photo courtesy of Bessemer State Technical College)

CHAPTER 2

WELDING TODAY

Although welding has been a key process for decades, it is by no means a technology of the past. Welding continues to play an important part in contemporary manufacturing efforts. As times have changed, so have the methods used in the practice of welding.

MAJOR WELDING PROCESSES

Welding offers a great deal of diversity. In fact, there are more than eighty different types of welding and allied processes, according to the American Welding Society. Some welders will use only one of these techniques while others will master many. The type of welding used depends on the equipment available, the job being performed, and the training of the individual welder.

If you become a welder, you will learn in-depth characteristics of one or more of these processes. Following is a brief description of the major welding techniques, which can be divided into several basic categories: arc welding, gas welding, resistance welding, soldering, brazing, solid-state welding, and other processes.

The most common welding processes, including arc and gas methods, fall within the umbrella of fusion welding. Here, heat is used to melt metals or other materials. The heat may be generated in any one of several ways. Once molten, the materials mix together and then become fused as they cool. Thus, two steel rods or beams, for example, can become essentially one piece of metal. In many cases, a filler material is also used in the process. This filler is heated, and as it becomes molten, it fills the joint between the original materials (called base metals or base materials).

Welding techniques vary in a number of ways. The most important differences include the way in which heat is produced, the type of fillers used (if any), the type of gas used for creating heat or providing shielding from contamination (if any), and the degree of automation.

Oxyfuel Gas Welding

If you had never tried welding but were asked to describe it, this is probably the methodology you would envision. In this type of welding, heat is produced by burning two gases: oxygen and another gas such as acetylene. The two gases are stored in heavy metal cylinders, which are connected to a welding torch by flexible hoses. The welder releases a stream of gas from each cylinder through a controlling device known as a regulator, and the two streams flow together inside the welding torch. As the gases begin to flow, the welder makes a spark or otherwise ignites the mixture, directs the flame to the area to be welded, and begins the welding process. This consists of using the flame to melt the base materials and then adding filler material as needed. All this is normally done by hand rather than through any kind of automated equipment.

The most common process of this type is oxyacetylene welding. This is often the preferred method of gas welding because burning acetylene produces a higher temperature than other gases used in welding. When burned after mixing with oxygen (which makes the gas burn more rapidly and at a higher temperature), acetylene can produce temperatures exceeding five thousand degrees Fahrenheit or three thousand degrees Celsius.

This type of welding can also be performed with other gases. Hydrogen, for example, can be mixed with oxygen in the same manner. Other gases such as methane, propane, and several others, which produce lower temperatures, are used for work related to welding such as metal cutting.

An advantage of oxyfuel welding is that it is a fairly simple process. Only a minimum of equipment is needed, and it can be moved about easily by a single welder. Thus, the process can be provided almost anywhere and is less expensive than more elaborate methods.

A disadvantage of oxyfuel welding is that it can be used for only certain types of jobs. Since the heat produced by burning gases is not as great as with some other methods, applications are limited to materials with relatively low melting points. In addition, the work proceeds more slowly than with many other methods. In general, it is not effective for large-scale jobs or those requiring speed or high volume.

Arc Welding

SMAW

One of the most common types of welding is shielded metal arc welding (often designated as SMAW). This is usually a manual process where the welder grasps a holder that contains a covered electrode used to create an electric arc. The welder turns on a welding machine which then causes electric current to flow to the electrode. As the electricity jumps across the gap between the tip of the electrode and the base material, it forms an arc that is hot enough to melt the electrode tip and the base material and form a weld.

The term *shielded* refers to a layer of gas that is released by the electrode covering when it becomes hot. This gas then protects the weld from being contaminated by the various elements of the atmosphere.

As the welder manipulates the electrode, it gradually melts away and provides filler material. Thus, electrodes must be continually replaced as a routine part of SMAW. Many different types of electrodes are available, varying in size, type of coating, usefulness in welding specific kinds of metals, and other characteristics. A major part of the experienced welder's job can be choosing the right electrode for the situation at hand.

GTAW

Another arc welding method is gas tungsten arc welding (GTAW). Here, a gas shield is provided not by a covered electrode as in SMAW but instead by a cylinder of gas. The gas is not burned in this case. It is an inert gas used to surround the area being welded and keep it from being contaminated by the different gases that make up the atmosphere. Inert gases (such as argon and helium) provide an effective shield because they do not normally react chemically with other elements.

In the GTAW process, a welding machine produces heat by creating an electric arc between an electrode made of tungsten and the area being welded. Tungsten has a high melting point; it does not become molten during GTAW welding. If filler material is needed to form the weld, it is periodically inserted into the arc by a two-hand technique.

This type of welding is also called TIG welding (for tungsten inert gas). It is often used for welding aluminum and stainless steel, among other metals.

GMAW

In gas metal arc welding (GMAW), the electrode, instead of being made of tungsten, is a continuous length of wire with a relatively low melting point, matching the properties of the metal to be welded. Generally, this wire is fed automatically by a welding machine, passing through a welding gun and serving as filler material at the point where the weld occurs.

In some cases, this process is completely automated, with the positioning of the welding gun also controlled by machine rather than by hand. In manual welding, the process of feeding wire is controlled by machine, but a welder manipulates the welding gun itself and directs the application of wire.

GMAW processes are also referred to as MIG welding (for metal inert gas). This type of welding is effective with a wide variety of materials.

Other types of arc welding include the following:

- Plasma Arc Welding (PAW). Here, an electric arc creates ''plasma'' by heating any one of several gases to an extremely high temperature, and then the heated gas is directed to a tightly controlled area where it melts the base metal to be welded.
- Flux Cored Arc Welding (FCAW). This process is similar to gas metal arc welding, with the difference that the electrode consists of hollow wire which is filled with a flexing material to provide shielding of the molten electrode and base metal during welding.
- Carbon Arc Welding (CAW). This welding technique uses electrodes made of carbon. In some cases, the arc is created between a carbon electrode and the base material, while in others the arc bridges two carbon electrodes.

- Submerged Arc Welding (SAW). As the name implies, submerged arc welding involves covering the arc during the welding process. This is accomplished by submerging the weld area under a granular flux. The welder does not actually see the area being welded but instead controls it by machine through an automatic or semiautomatic process.

Resistance Welding

Resistance welding (RW) is an electric welding process. Its basis is that an electric current forced to pass through a poor conductor is converted to heat by the resistance of the medium. In resistance welding, electricity is passed through two pieces of metal in contact to heat the metal at the interface, and the two pieces are pressed together after they have fused. Once cooled, the parts have become welded together.

Employers who use the resistance method may assign welders to several different types of resistance welding equipment. These include:

- Flash welding (FW), where parts being welded are brought into contact and briefly separated to create an electric arc, and then quickly pressed together, causing sparks, or "flashes," for which the process is named.
- Percussion welding (PEW), where parts are percussively forced together during or immediately following an electrical discharge.

- Resistance spot welding (RSW), in which opposing electrodes heat one spot at the facing surfaces between metal sheets to be joined, with heat supplied by electric current.
- Resistance seam welding (RSW), a process using a series of overlapping spot welds to produce a watertight or airtight seam.
- Resistance projection welding (RPW), where projections, embossments, or intersections are raised on the work parts to localize predetermined weld points.
- Upset welding (UW), in which pieces of metal are clamped together and joined through the resistance to electric current.

Brazing

Brazing is similar to welding, but it differs from most welding processes in that the objects or materials being joined are not melted. Instead, a different substance with a lower melting point from the materials to be joined is melted and used to join them together. The basic concept of brazing might be compared to using glue to join together two objects.

For example, brazing can be used to join together copper tubes or pipes. A filler metal with a relatively low melting point such as brass (an alloy of zinc and copper) is heated with a torch and applied to the copper pieces, joining them together as the alloy melts and then solidifies.

Although heat is used, only the filler material becomes molten. As a result, brazing can be used to join materials that must be treated delicately (such as gems or jewelry) as well as copper pipes, aluminum, and many other materials.

Soldering

Soldering is somewhat similar to brazing. A major difference is that a still lower temperature is used in the process, meaning quite different filler materials are applied. In many cases, the filler is an alloy of tin and lead. Such an alloy melts easily and requires only a simple device known as a soldering iron for application. Many people learn soldering as their first exposure to any welding-related process, often in connection with work in electronics. In industrial applications, soldering is used for jobs ranging from joining tubes inside an air conditioner to attaching parts of sophisticated electronic devices.

Although soldering is readily done by hand, many industrial soldering jobs are handled automatically with several types of soldering machines.

Solid-State Welding

Until just a few generations ago, one of the most important persons in any community was the blacksmith. Blacksmiths were among the precursors of today's welders, for as a part of their jobs, they were able to join pieces of metal together. Blacksmiths learned to heat metal until it became more malleable (even though it did not melt) and then hammered the pieces together. This form of forge welding is still practiced by blacksmiths today, although the craft may soon become a forgotten skill. The same approach is also used in more modern manufacturing processes, where special furnaces heat metal devices that are then fused together.

Even when metals are not heated, some can be joined together through a process known as cold welding. Softer metals such as aluminum, lead, silver, and gold can be fused together by applying sufficient pressure.

Several other types of solid-state welding are also used in a variety of applications including diffusion welding, friction welding, and a number of variations.

NEW TYPES OF WELDING

In any area of technology advancements occur, and welding is no different. During recent years, several new welding processes have been introduced, and more can be expected in the future.

Lasers

One of the most interesting of the new processes is laser beam welding (LBW). As the name indicates, this type of welding depends on the highly amplified beams of light (lasers) which are now used commonly in a number of applications. Although many laser applications depend on the beams passing through or bouncing harmlessly off material (as with the scanning devices used at checkout counters in grocery stores), for use in welding, laser beams are quite intensive and capable of producing great heat. With a laser welding machine (a complex and tremendously expensive piece of equipment), a tightly controlled beam of light is produced that can melt many metals quickly.

A plus for LBW is that it can be very precise. The area heated is very tiny, resulting in the potential for extremely accurate work. This can be important in scientific and highly technical applications.

Electron Beams

Another innovative process is electron beam welding (EBW). In this process, a stream of electrons (charged particles that are one of the basic parts of atoms) is produced by heating a filament. The high-velocity electrons are focused near the point to be welded, which is usually placed inside a chamber where all the air has been removed to create a vacuum. This produces heat which is so intense portions of the metal are vaporized and condense on the opposite wall of the "vapor hole." The beam pierces through the metal as it progresses along the weld joint.

Ultrasonics

Unlike most welding techniques, ultrasonic welding does not use or produce heat. Instead, the welder operates a machine which produces intense sound vibrations. These high-frequency sound waves break up the surface of the materials being joined together and then cause them to fuse.

Ultrasonic welding is particularly useful in producing electronic devices and components. It is also used extensively in packaging food and beverages.

Other Advancements

Other welding processes offer their own unique features. Some differ substantially from traditional welding methods while others combine features of two or more processes. Such processes as electrogas welding, electroslag welding, friction welding, and diffusion welding also provide alternative approaches for accomplishing various welding tasks. A complete listing of the major welding processes is provided later in this chapter.

RELATED TECHNOLOGIES

The function of welders is to join materials together for the purposes of construction or repair. The basic skills and aptitudes required in welding, however, can also be applied to the cutting of metal and other metal-working functions.

A variety of welding methods may be employed by welders or by persons who specialize in cutting as opposed to welding (with the difference being that welding generally entails joining materials together while cutting involves just the opposite). Of course these functions can be closely related, as when workers must cut off a section of metal from a larger piece and then weld it to another. On the other hand, cutting may consist entirely of taking apart materials or structures, depending on the job.

At any rate, a variety of techniques may be used in cutting. Thermal cutting techniques depend on using oxygen or electric arc processes while other methods include laser beam cutting and electron beam cutting.

Still other processes related to welding include thermal spraying (a method of metal resurfacing) and an alternative method of joining materials known as adhesive bonding.

THE DIVERSITY OF WELDING PROCESSES

The previous pages have provided a brief overview of some of the most important welding processes and those that are used most commonly today. Many other related processes, however, also have their own individual applications.

Following is a listing of welding and related processes as reported by the American Welding Society (AWS). This information is adapted with permission from the AWS publication *Welding Terms and Definitions*.

ARC WELDING

atomic hydrogen welding	AHW
bare metal arc welding	BMAW
carbon arc welding	CAW
gas	CAW-G
shielded	CAW-S
twin	CAW-T
electrogas welding	EGW
flux cored arc welding	FCAW
gas metal arc welding	GMAW
pulsed arc	GMAW-P
short circuiting arc	GMAW-S
gas tungsten arc welding	GTAW
pulsed arc	GTAW-P
plasma arc welding	PAW
shielded metal arc welding	SMAW
stud arc welding	SW
submerged arc welding	SAW
series	SAW-S

OXYFUEL GAS WELDING (OFW)

air acetylene welding	AAW
oxyacetylene welding	OAW
oxyhydrogen welding	OHW
pressure gas welding	PGW

RESISTANCE WELDING (RW)

flash welding	FW
high frequency resistance welding	HFRW
percussion welding	PEW
projection welding	RPW

resistance seam welding	RSEW
resistance spot welding	RSW
upset welding	UW

SOLID-STATE WELDING (SSW)

coextrusion welding	CEW
cold welding	CW
diffusion welding	DFW
explosion welding	EXW
forge welding	FOW
friction welding	FRW
hot pressure welding	HPW
roll welding	ROW
ultrasonic welding	USW

BRAZING (B)

arc brazing	AB
block brazing	BB
diffusion brazing	DFB
dip brazing	DB
flow brazing	FLB
furnace brazing	FB
induction brazing	IB
infrared brazing	IRB
resistance brazing	RB
torch brazing	TB
twin carbon arc blazing	TCAB

SOLDERING (S)

dip soldering	DS

furnace soldering	FS
induction soldering	IS
infrared soldering	IRS
iron soldering	INS
resistance soldering	RS
torch soldering	TS
wave soldering	WS

OTHER WELDING

electron beam welding	EBW
high vacuum	EBW-HV
medium vacuum	EBW-MV
nonvacuum	EBW-NV
electroslag welding	ESW
flow welding	FLOW
induction welding	IW
laser beam welding	LBW
thermit welding	TW

PROCESSES ALLIED TO WELDING

THERMAL SPRAYING (THSP)

electric arc spraying	EASP
flame spraying	FLSP
plasma spraying	PSP

ADHESIVE BONDING (ABD)

OXYGEN CUTTING (OC)

chemical flux cutting	FOC
metal powder cutting	POC
oxyfuel gas cutting	OFC
oxyacetylene cutting	OFC-A
oxyhydrogen cutting	OFC-H

oxynatural gas cutting	OFC-N
oxypropane cutting	OFC-P
oxygen cutting	AOC
oxygen lance cutting	LOC

ARC CUTTING (AC)

air carbon arc cutting	AAC
carbon arc cutting	CAC
gas metal arc cutting	GMAC
gas tungsten arc cutting	GTAC
metal arc cutting	MAC
plasma arc cutting	PAC
shielded metal arc cutting	SMAC

OTHER CUTTING

electron beam cutting	EBC
laser beam cutting	LBC

At first glance, such a long list of welding processes may be a little intimidating. All of this can seem pretty complicated. But when you consider the following points, the depth and breadth of the welding field can seem substantially less overpowering.

You will need to learn only a few of these processes, or perhaps just one. Many welding jobs focus on just one type of welding work. Unless you change jobs frequently or simply want to learn all kinds of processes, you probably will not be required to master a wide range of techniques.

There is always more to learn. Because the field is so diverse, the opportunity to learn more always exists. This can provide a great way to avoid boredom on the job as well as to advance yourself professionally.

Welding always offers room for new technologies and new materials. Because welding grows and changes along with other technologies, it does not become easily outdated. This is an extremely important point for those concerned about job security in future years. By changing and growing, the welding field remains a strong, viable area of employment.

CHAPTER 3

WHAT WELDERS DO

As the previous chapter illustrates, the work performed by welders can vary widely. Welders construct all kinds of items. They may use a simple welding torch or a complex machine costing over a million dollars. They may work on their own or in teams, entirely by hand or only with automated equipment. One welder may do the same kind of work day in and day out while another may switch frequently from one job assignment to another.

While persons employed in welding may work in diverse environments, they share a number of common factors. All welders use their particular skills to construct or repair buildings, equipment, or other man-made structures. In most cases this means working with metal, although in recent years welding has also expanded into plastics and other materials. In any case, most welders approach their jobs in similar ways, and they work within a few basic areas. Although one welder may specialize in using equipment that is unfamiliar to another, the basic kind of work done is quite similar from one industry to another, from East Coast to West Coast, whether in urban or rural areas. Even in other countries, the tasks performed by welders tend to be somewhat similar, especially when grouped within basic areas of welding technology as described in the previous chapter.

WHERE WELDERS WORK

Building Construction

If you see a new house being constructed in your neighborhood, the workers probably will not include welders. Although some of the basic components may have involved welding (for example, the construction of furnaces or certain kinds of plumbing fixtures), other work is performed by different craftspersons.

For other types of buildings, though, welders may play an important role in the construction process. For example, a high-rise office building will not be made of wood and brick but instead is more likely to be constructed largely of steel and reinforced concrete. Much of the steel superstructure of the building will be assembled by welders. Before any concrete can be poured, welders or other metalworkers must connect beams and weld together the steel reinforcing rods.

The same is true in the construction of other large buildings. A gymnasium may be built of any number of materials, but a basic part of its construction will be metal beams and various elements of the basic support structure. A single-level manufacturing building may be constructed of corrugated metal designed for fast construction and a "no-frills" work environment—with welders performing much of the basic assembly. Or a car dealership may be expanding into a new series of buildings including a new showroom, repair shop, and office facilities—all containing substantial quantities of metal components that must be assembled by welders.

The fact that welding is an important facet of the construction industry means that opportunities for welders abound in all kinds of settings. In virtually every city in America, a quick trip across town will reveal a number of buildings under construction. The same is true in suburban areas and even many rural communities, especially where industrial parks are located. And many of these construction jobs call for the work of welders.

An interesting aspect of building construction is that many structures are partially or entirely prefabricated. In these cases, welders and other workers may turn out a variety of building components (or even entire structures such as storage buildings) without ever leaving their shop environment.

On the other hand, working on the site of a new building can provide an interesting challenge for the welder. Persons employed in such positions often cite the change in routine from one building project to the next as one of the major assets of their jobs.

Bridge/Highway Construction

The next time you take a drive in a car or truck, pay special attention to the presence of metal within the highway systems you are travelling on. While at first glance it appears that highways are made entirely of concrete or asphalt, almost every road construction project also involves the placement of metal in a variety of locations—from guard rails to huge bridges spanning rivers or valleys. In addition, many smaller bridges are built into roads that are not particularly obvious to the traveler.

The construction of bridges represents one of the most intensive and important applications of modern welding processes. Welders help construct long bridges for interstate highways and state roads, small bridges crossing country streams, and everything in between. With the growth in population and the building of new highways, bridge construction continues to be a major area in which welders work. In addition, bridges are not permanent—even though they may last for decades—and the repair and replacement of worn-out bridges especially calls for the help of welders.

Automotive Industry

The American automobile industry is one of the largest business endeavors of any kind in the world. Every year, according to the U.S. Department of Commerce, more than eight million passenger cars are manufactured along with over three million trucks and buses. In the manufacturing of all these automobiles, welders play an important part. Since most cars are largely made of metal, welding is an essential step in making most auto components.

(Frequently, the welding process in car and truck construction is an automated one. Many workers in large auto plants become operators of welding machines.) Although this work is important and yields good wages and benefits, it may not require in-depth knowledge of a variety of welding techniques.) This may be seen as an advantage for those who enjoy mastering a single job and then sticking to it or as a disadvantage to those who prefer a great deal of variety in the workplace.

As technology continues to advance, more steps in the construction of automobiles are being carried out by robots and other devices. Nevertheless, a welding robot needs to be supervised by a knowledgeable welder. In addition, a greater reliance on plastics and composite materials may reduce the need for welding in basic car construction.

The auto repair industry represents another area where welding is important. While this is largely the province of auto mechanics, mechanics welcome the speed and simplicity of welding. For example, a broken radiator or exhaust pipe may need to be repaired, with welding being the most practical method. Or say that an individual wants to add a hitch to his or her car for towing a camper, boat, or trailer. A hitch for this purpose may be constructed or adapted by a worker who specializes in welding such parts.

Work in auto repairing is where some people first learn welding. In many cases that can be the starting point for a career in other types of welding applications.

Shipbuilding

Of course there are not nearly as many ships produced annually as cars or airplanes, but the huge amount of work involved in constructing a ship creates a big demand for the skills of welders. In fact, shipbuilding is one of the major areas of employment for welders.

Compared with the manufacture of planes or autos, the scope and scale of shipbuilding are vastly larger. Welders may be involved for months or years in the construction of a single ship. Instead of the finished product being an auto weighing less than two tons, the end result may be a merchant vessel or naval ship covering the length of a football field and weighing thousands of tons. Building a supertanker or aircraft carrier, for example, may seem more like constructing a small city than assembling a means of transportation.

At any rate, the large amounts of metal used in building ships means that the work of welders is required in a major way. Many welders spend all of their time solely in this industry.

Naturally, most welding jobs related to shipbuilding are found in coastal areas such as the Norfolk-Hampton Roads area in Virginia. Persons interested in working as welders in this industry should either live within commuting distance of major ship construction facilities or be willing to relocate to such an area on a temporary or permanent basis.

This applies to the actual assembly of ships but not necessarily to all their components. As with many other industries, companies that build ships rely on other firms for many elements of the finished product. In many cases, this means welding jobs at inland locations are also involved in shipbuilding. For instance, key ship parts may be built at a factory far from the ocean and then transported to the ship construction site. So at least indirectly, welding jobs based on ship construction may be obtained at various locations around the country.

Too, some vessels are not designed to travel at sea but rather on inland waterways. Large barges that carry coal and other items on waterways such as the Ohio River and Mississippi River may be constructed far from any ocean but involve many of the same kinds of welding work as in ocean-going ship construction.

Aircraft Construction

Like cars and ships, airplanes are constructed largely of metal parts, and the aerospace industry relies heavily on the work of welders and other metal workers. Welders help construct jumbo jets and other commercial airliners, mid-sized planes for commercial and private use, and many small airplanes and helicopters. In addition, they help meet the needs of the armed forces by building military aircraft, often under the employment of a private corporation that has been awarded a defense contract.

Because of the stringent safety measures observed in the aircraft industry, the work performed by welders in this area provides special challenges. Welders employed in this capacity must provide consistently good work that meets corporate and federal safety and performance standards.

The sheer beauty and excitement many people feel when working with modern flying machines can also be enjoyed by those who build them. After all, it is difficult not to feel a sense of accomplishment in helping construct craft that can fly faster than sound, hover virtually motionless just off the ground, or perform any of the other functions possible with various types of airplanes and helicopters. As a result, working in the aircraft industry can be one of the more glamorous welding careers.

OTHER WORK ENVIRONMENTS

Individuals who have been trained as welders can also, in many cases, find employment in related areas. This might mean working for a period of years as a welder and then changing to a related area. Or it might mean studying welding to learn basic concepts and then following a career in one of the following areas.

Welding Sales

One related career is the sale of welding products. While a salesperson need not necessarily be a trained welder, men and women with some experience in welding can be expected to have an edge in understanding the products they sell and the particular needs of customers. Thus, a career track that a welder might follow is branching off into the sale of equipment and supplies for the welding industry.

Pick up any telephone directory and look in the yellow pages under ''welding equipment and supplies,'' and you will see a number of companies. The Norfolk-Portsmouth area in Virginia, for example, shows fourteen different welding supply/equipment firms in the yellow pages alone, not counting those who choose to pass up this form of advertising. In this or any other city, the range of sales positions varies from clerks working in a branch of a large company to persons running their own small businesses.

A career in sales is certainly not for everyone, but it might be a possibility, especially if you can exhibit (or develop) most of the following characteristics:

- A basic understanding of welding concepts and practices
- Good oral communication skills
- A genuine liking for working with people
- A high degree of self-motivation and the ability to work independently without a great deal of supervision

- Good organizational and record-keeping abilities
- Honesty
- A willingness to travel frequently (if required, as some—but not all—sales jobs require travel)

Of course, different people handle sales positions in different ways, and there is no single formula for success. But if you can demonstrate these kinds of qualities, welding-related sales work may represent a challenging career alternative.

Teaching

If you become a skilled welder, one option worth exploring is teaching. Teaching is certainly not for everyone, but it can provide a rewarding career for some men and women who have mastered welding techniques to the degree where they would be in a realistic position to teach such skills to others.

A quick look at appendix B will show you that hundreds of trade schools and colleges offer programs in welding. In addition, many vocational high schools offer similar programs. In each case, welding instructors are needed to teach the various courses offered.

The requirements for obtaining welding teaching positions vary depending on the type of school, local standards, rules established by accrediting agencies, and other factors. In some cases, a four-year degree is required, but in others, experience and technical knowledge can be substituted for some educational credentials. If you are interested, check with the welding department, personnel office, or other appropriate official at any school that offers welding and ask what is expected of persons desiring to teach. You can then keep these requirements in mind as you acquire welding skills and other background.

One of the nice features of teaching is that it is not necessarily an "either-or" proposition. In other words, becoming a teacher does not mean you must give up welding work in other settings. Many welding teachers serve as instructors on a part-time basis only, teaching evening or other classes to expand their horizons and earn some extra income. Similarly, many full-time welding instructors perform direct welding work on a part-time or summer basis when it does not conflict with their educational duties.

Business Owner

Some welders opt to start their own businesses rather than work for other employers. This may mean operating what is sometimes called a job shop, where welders perform various welding jobs for individuals, small businesses, or even large companies that contract out such work instead of hiring their own staff of welders.

Another option is to own or manage a business that specializes in welding equipment or supplies. Every company or individual conducting welding work must obtain the necessary equipment and supplies, ranging from complex welding machines to consumable supplies such as the various gases used in oxyfuel and other welding processes. The resultant demand means that a continuing market exists for firms specializing in such products.

A degree or diploma in welding is not necessary to manage a business of this type, but basic knowledge of welding practices is essential. In addition, an understanding of the elements of business management is vital.

The Military

While most welding jobs are found with civilian companies, the skills of welders are also in significant demand within the armed services. An advantage, if you are selected, is that the military will provide the needed training at no cost to you. Such training can be applied not only during time spent in the armed services but also in civilian life following military service. Not only is the training itself free, but you earn normal military pay while being trained. Such a combination can be hard to beat.

Naturally, all of this depends on your ability to fit into military life and adapt to its particular requirements. Some people thrive in the military, while others hate it. The situation all depends on your own goals, career preferences, and basic personality. To find out more about the options provided by military service, contact a recruiter for any one of the armed forces. Then take some time to weigh things carefully before making any kind of commitment.

JOB TITLES

The U.S. Department of Labor lists the following job titles related to welding:

Arc Cutter
Gas-Tungsten Arc Cutter
Plasma Arc Cutter
Brazer
Assembler Brazer
Controlled Atmospheric Furnace Brazer
Crawler Torch Blazer
Electronic Brazer
Furnace Brazer
Furnace Brazer Helper
Induction Brazer Helper
Induction Brazer
Production Line Brazer
Repair and Salvage Brazer
Resistance Brazer
Brazing-Furnace Feeder
Brazing-Machine Feeder
Brazing-Machine Operator
Brazing-Machine Operator Helper
Brazing-Machine Setter
Hand Burner
Burning-Machine Operator
Certified Welder
Gas Cutter

Electronic-Eye-Thermal-Cutting-Machine Operator
Flame-Brazing-Machine Operator
Flame-Cutting-Machine Operator
Flame-Cutting-Machine-Operator Helper
Flame Gouger
Flame Planer
Flame Scarfer
Flash-Welding-Machine Operator
Flash Brusher
Gas-Cutting-Machine Operator
Hydrogen Brazing-Furnace Operator
Laser-Beam Cutter
Laser-Beam-Machine Operator
Lead Burner
Lead-Burner Apprentice
Lead-Burner Supervisor
Machine Feeder
Machine Helper
Magnetic-Thermal-Cutting-Machine Operator
Percussion-Welding-Machine Operator
Performance-Test Inspector
Plasma-Cutting-Machine Operator
Production-Welding-Machine Operator
Cylinder Heads Repairer
Welding Equipment Repairer
Induction-Heating-Equipment Setter
Side-Seam Tender
Slag Scraper
Solderer-Assembler

Solderer-Dipper
Electronic Solderer
Furnace Solderer
Induction Solderer
Production Line Solderer
Silver Solderer
Torch Solderer
Soldering-Machine Feeder
Soldering-Machine Operator
Soldering-Machine Operator Helper
Hand Thermal Cutter
Thermal-Cutter Helper
Thermal-Cutting-Tracer-Machine Operator
Torch Brazer
Torch Cutter
Upset-Welding-Machine Operator
Acetylene Welder
Arc Welder Apprentice
Arc Welder
Gas Welder
Gas Welder Apprentice
Combination Welder
Combination Welder Apprentice
Experimental Welder
Explosion Welder
Welder-Fitter
Welder-Fitter Apprentice
Arc Welder-Fitter
Gas Welder-Fitter

Flux-Cored Arc Welder
Gas-Metal Arc Welder
Gas-Tungsten Arc Welder
Gun Welder
Submerged Arc Hand Welder
Welder Helper
Oxyacetylene Welder
Oxyhydrogen Welder
Plasma Arc Welder
Production Line Welder
Production Line Arc Welder
Repair Welder
Electron-Beam Machine Welder Setter
Resistance Machine Welder Setter
Shielded-Metal Arc Welder
Structural Repair Welder
Tack Welder
Tool and Die Welder
Welding-Machine Feeder
Arc Welding-Machine Operator
Electro-Gas Welding-Machine Operator
Electron Beam Welding-Machine Operator
Electroslag Welding-Machine Operator
Friction Welding-Machine Operator
Gas Welding-Machine Operator
Gas-Metal Arc Welding-Machine Operator
Gas-Tungsten Arc Welding Machine Operator
Welding-Machine-Operator Helper
Submerged Arc Welding-Machine Operator

Thermit Welding-Machine Operator
Ultrasonic Welding-Machine Operator
Welding-Machine Tender
Welding Tester
Weld Inspector

TOOLS, SUPPLIES, AND EQUIPMENT
USED IN WELDING

A requirement in any welding job is the ability to use basic equipment necessary to carry out various welding tasks. While every person employed in welding will not necessarily need to know how to use every type of equipment available, most welders work routinely with a wide range of tools, supplies, and welding equipment. Following is a list of some of the most frequently used items:

- Goggles—used for basic eye protection
- Protective gloves—used to protect hands and wrists
- Safety shoes—shoes containing steel toes or other safety features
- Igniter—used to create sparks to ignite flammable gases
- Gas cylinders—metal containers, usually made of steel, that contain compressed gases such as oxygen or acetylene
- Cylinder valves—devices used to release or restrict the flow of gas from a cylinder

- Welding booth—a confined area for use in welding; walls keep sparks and metal spattering from surrounding area
- Welding torch—a basic device, often hand held, from which heat is applied directly to the area being welded
- Welding positioner—a device used to position and hold materials while welding takes place
- Various types of welding machines

A DAY IN THE LIFE OF A WELDER

Perhaps there is no such thing as a typical day in the life of a welder. But to give you a more complete picture of what a career in welding might be like, here is an overview of one day's routine as followed by two persons employed as welders.

Mining Equipment Welder

Maria works for a company that makes mining equipment. She was very nervous during her first day on the job eight months ago, fearing not only that she might make some critical mistake but that she might not be accepted by the four other welders working for the same company, all of whom were male. But her co-workers were helpful and cooperative, especially when she demonstrated that she could handle the job readily.

Most of Maria's time is taken up in helping construct various kinds of mining equipment, including huge automatic mining machines known as continuous miners. Her daily work routine begins at 8:00 A.M., when she clocks in and picks up where she finished working the previous day. Unlike many employees in other manufacturing firms who work rotating shifts, Maria and the co-workers in her unit work eight-hour, daytime assignments most of the year. Occasionally when the company has received a high volume of business and production levels must be increased, Maria and other employees are asked to work overtime, which may consist of evening work or a Saturday shift. For such work she receives extra pay, calculated at one-and-a-half times the normal hourly wage. In most instances, she welcomes the chance to earn the extra income.

Maria's working environment consists of a large building containing a variety of working stations, conveyor belts, and other components. During her first few days on the job, she found the area to be noisy and somewhat inhibiting due to all the activity, but before long, she adjusted to the situation and now finds it a normal and acceptable part of her routine.

Along with other workers, Maria takes a fifteen-minute break during the morning and again during the afternoon, along with forty-five minutes at lunch. On some days she eats in the company snack bar or a fast food restaurant across the street while other times she brings a packed lunch from home.

By the end of a typical day, Maria may be physically tired, but she feels good about her work. It gives her a special feeling of satisfaction to see a finished piece of complex equipment and know that she played an important part in constructing it. When she stops to consider her role as a welder, she feels glad she chose this career.

Welding in Saudi Arabia

For Scott, a job in welding has supported a desire he had always had to see places other than his home state of Alabama. He particularly enjoyed a two-year stint working on a pipeline in Alaska, has worked in California and New Mexico, and now is facing a brand-new adventure: working in Saudi Arabia.

Unlike Maria, Scott spends most of the time working outdoors rather than inside a factory. This has involved a great deal of variety, ranging from frigid wintertime work to the heat of the Saudi Arabian desert. In his current role, he is helping build the towers and other structures needed for a new petrochemical plant.

In addition to the experience of living and working in a foreign country, Scott benefits from the extremely high wages paid to skilled workers in this setting. Along with hourly wages, he earns bonuses, living expenses, and support for travel. A disadvantage is that he is far from friends and family in the United States, but the assignment is temporary, and he plans to return within the next two years.

Typical Tasks

Of course many welders work in jobs far different from those of Maria or Scott, but each position has its own features and responsibilities. Some typical tasks performed by welders holding different kinds of job include:

- Welding joints on the deck of a partially completed ship
- Connecting a steel beam to the main structure of an interstate highway bridge
- Welding components of a cooling system for a new nuclear power plant
- Joining together components of washing machines in an appliance factory
- Helping assemble steel storage buildings in a small firm specializing in constructing storage units and selling them to homeowners
- Operating a welding machine in a truck assembly plant
- Welding pipes in a hospital expansion project
- Repairing broken pipes in an office building
- Assembling components of an airplane

In addition, persons employed as welders may perform other functions as a part of their jobs that do not entail welding itself. Examples on a given day for some welders might include:

- Attending a training session on safety
- Traveling from one work site to another
- Ordering or obtaining welding supplies
- Helping orient a new employee

• Attending a class or seminar on new welding techniques

WELDING SAFELY

A major responsibility of welders is maintaining safe work practices. After all, welding is serious business involving potentially dangerous materials and situations. If proper safety procedures are not understood and followed carefully, serious injury and property damage can result.

For example, consider the danger posed by burns. Most welding processes generate intense heat, usually at least several times hotter than the highest temperature reached with a kitchen stove or outdoor grill. If these relatively "cold" temperatures can sizzle a steak, just imagine what a welding torch can do to your hand or arm! And hot metal or other heated material can also cause a nasty burn.

Another possibility is an explosion. Flammable gases can cause explosions if mishandled, endangering not just one individual but nearby workers as well.

Electric shock is another danger area. As an essential ingredient in many welding processes, electricity is commonly utilized by welders. At the same time, its misuse can have devastating results. Failure to use proper safety procedures in dealing with electricity may cause serious accidents.

Welders must also guard against other types of accidents. Eye injuries, inhalation of gases, abrasions, and other problems also loom as possible dangers to anyone working in welding.

What all this means is not that people should shy away from welding careers because an accident might happen, for most jobs entail some possibility of accident. Rather, recognize that paying attention to safety is a major responsibility of every welder. Men and women employed in the field need to learn the safest ways to complete welding tasks and then constantly observe appropriate caution in performing their work.

Safety-related responsibilities of welders may include:

- Mastering basic safety techniques within the context of the welding field
- Regularly using equipment designed to enhance safety such as goggles, face plates, and other protective items
- Continually checking equipment to make sure it is in proper and safe working order
- Observing special caution in handling combustible materials and electrical equipment.
- Refraining from using drugs or alcohol during working hours or before reporting to work
- Reading and retaining safety-related information provided by employers or equipment manufacturers
- Participating in seminars or special training programs designed to enhance safety in the workplace
- Keeping work areas free of debris, equipment that is not being used, and other clutter
- Promoting safe working habits with fellow welders

- Keeping safety in mind all the time rather than just giving it occasional attention

QUESTIONS TO ASK YOURSELF

If the life of a welder sounds interesting and you want to pursue this field in further detail, ask yourself some basic details such as the following:

Do I have the right aptitudes? Just as everyone is not cut out to function effectively as a butcher, accountant, fighter pilot, or professional baseball player, every individual does not possess the right traits to work successfully or contentedly as a welder. If you have patience, are attentive to detail, and have good manual skills, a welding career may be a smart idea. If you lack these basic traits most welders possess, on the other hand, you might want to consider another area.

Am I dependable? Companies that employ welders need personnel who are dependable. Can you get to work regularly and promptly? Will you work constantly at your daily tasks, placing the importance of the work to be done above coffee breaks, frequent chatting with other employees, and other personal interests? An affirmative answer to questions such as these is necessary for success in virtually any welding job.

Perhaps even more importantly, employees and customers must be able to depend on the quality of your work.

It is not enough merely to go through the motions in a job as complex as welding. You must care sufficiently about your work to do a good job, day in and day out. Too much will be riding on the work involved for you to lack dependability.

Do I have the necessary physical traits? People with all kinds of physical characteristics can become effective welders. It is not necessary to be over six feet tall and blessed with bulging muscles, for example, even though physical strength can be an asset in any job involving the movement and positioning of sometimes heavy objects. Individuals who are small in stature or not particularly strong can still function effectively by learning efficient techniques for making the most of whatever strength they do possess.

Some specific physical capabilities are needed, however, and it is wise to ask yourself if they can be found in your own basic profile. Good eyesight, for example, is a must. If poor eyesight is corrected by glasses or contact lenses, of course, it presents no problem. But to perform basic welding work, you must be able to see clearly and be able to distinguish minute details in the materials with which you are working.

Physical stamina is also an asset. Welders usually work at least eight hours a day, often standing or crouching. The ability to put in the required hours, which may involve varying degrees of physical exertion, is a routine consideration.

It also helps to possess a good measure of dexterity. This might range from having nimble fingers to being able to climb ladders, squeeze into tight spots, or otherwise move about as the job requires. Depending on the type of job they are doing, welders may find themselves reaching above their heads, lying on their backs, or climbing ladders or scaffolding.

A steady hand is also necessary. Without this attribute, any kind of manual welding will be difficult to perform well.

Am I willing to go to school? To become a welder, you will almost certainly need to undergo some type of training. Although it may be possible to learn the basics of welding under some type of self-teaching situation, it is unlikely. At the very least, most people need some rather detailed training obtained on the job. More frequently, some kind of formal training is needed to land your first job in welding.

Such training can be obtained in a number of ways, including the following:

- High school vocational programs
- Trade and technical schools
- Community and junior colleges
- Technical colleges
- Industry-sponsored training programs
- Government-sponsored training programs
- Apprenticeships
- Military training programs

A description of the various educational options is provided in chapter 4. Each type of program has its own advantages and disadvantages, but the essential point to establish is your basic willingness to participate in the necessary training. Such a commitment will take up your time and energy, ranging perhaps from reading textbooks and manuals or attending lecture sessions to participating in laboratory/shop training where you will obtain your first hands-on welding experience. It may also include a financial commitment on your part, requiring you to pay tuition or other educational costs. And it will also mean subjecting yourself once again to the overall role of being a student and all that accompanies student status. If you have not enjoyed going to school in the past, this can represent something of a sacrifice in that you are once again subjecting yourself to the control of teachers and other elements of an educational organization.

A plus, however, is that welding programs tend to be short and well defined. Studying welding does not involve going to college for four years and taking a wide variety of courses that may not seem to relate to the "real world." On the contrary, most welding programs can be completed in a few weeks or months, with the longest programs lasting about two years. Because of their occupational emphasis, training programs in welding tend to be as short as reasonably possible and very practical in their approach. This means less time spent studying unrelated material, fewer hours listening to lectures, and more time spent actually practicing welding techniques. As a result, many students, often including those who have not previously enjoyed school, find that instructional time passes quickly and that their experiences as welding students are both challenging and rewarding.

The educational options available to any one person are often a matter of geography. In some areas, several types of welding programs may be offered. In others, a single option may be available. In this case, selection of a training program may mean simply going to one school in your home area that teaches welding. Or it might mean moving temporarily to another city to complete an appropriate program.

Does a long-term career in welding meet my economic and social needs? Any career selection carries with it some implications regarding life-styles outside the job as well as within the career itself. For example, the salary or wages earned will play a direct role in fundamental matters such as what kind of housing you can afford or the kind of car you drive. Similarly, job requirements such as shift work, travel, and other factors will influence your daily life in many ways.

Before pursuing a career in welding, make certain that you understand just what type of life-style it will support. Make certain you check out income possibilities (covered in more detail in a later chapter), fringe benefits, opportunities for advancement, and job stability. In thinking ahead, it is vital to match your own particular needs and expectations with the realities of employment in welding.

CHAPTER 4

GETTING TRAINED

(In most cases, you will need to complete a special training program to learn the skills required to obtain a job in welding. Although a number of alternative ways to master these skills exist (for example, see the information on special training programs in chapter 5), the most common path is to enroll in a welding program offered by a school or college.) This will involve making educational plans beyond your current situation, choosing a school, and then successfully negotiating the appropriate training process.

PLANNING AHEAD

To prepare for a welding career, make certain you plan ahead to obtain the right educational background. In the process, ask yourself questions such as these:

• What schools offer welding programs in my area?

- Am I willing to go away to school, or would I prefer to stay home or close by?
- Am I in a hurry to finish?
- Which is best for me, a trade school, or a two-year college?
- How much will it cost?
- How will I pay for it?
- What steps should I take to make certain I succeed?

By carefully considering such questions before you actually enroll in a welding program, you can increase the odds that the program will turn out to be the right experience for you. This kind of advance planning can help you avoid mistakes that can be costly in terms of time, money, and overall career success.

CHOOSING A SCHOOL

As a first step, you will need to select a school that offers a welding program. This can be an easy decision or a difficult one, depending on the factors taken into consideration.

If the choice is too easy, though, it may not be a smart one. Just signing up for the first welding program you hear about or the one closest to your home can be a big mistake. Taking time to select the right school can mean the difference between a good program or a mediocre one, or in obtaining a diploma that is widely respected by employers as opposed to one that is viewed with skepticism or disdain. Choosing the right school can also save you a great deal of money.

This is not always easy, but it can be done if you take your time and know what to look for. Unfortunately, almost every school makes claims about itself in an effort to attract students, so you will need to do more than simply read promotional literature or listen to the sales pitch of a recruiter.

Types of Schools

As a basic step in considering any institution, make sure you understand exactly what kind of school it is. Depending on several key characteristics, a school offering welding courses may be operating as a trade school, a technical institute, a technical college, or a junior or community college. Each type offers certain advantages and disadvantages, and you should be aware of them before enrolling in any particular institution.

For instance, a trade school normally offers training programs on a short-term basis in one or more occupational-technical subjects. A typical school of this type offering welding may also teach other subjects such as computer repair, word processing, and diesel mechanics. On the other hand, it probably will not require students to take courses such as foreign languages, advanced math classes, or English courses. When students graduate, they do not receive a college degree but instead earn a certificate or diploma.

You can also enroll in welding courses in a two-year college that might be designated as a junior college, community college, or technical college. In many cases the course covered will be much the same as in a trade school, with graduates earning a diploma or certificate (usually in a year or less) rather than a degree. In some other cases, though, students complete the equivalent of two years of studies and wind up with an actual college degree, called an associate degree. Students who earn such degrees must take classes in other areas in addition to welding such as English, history, technical writing, or psychology. Earning any two-year degree will mean completing a few of these courses which are considered a general education requirement for virtually all college students.

It is also important to realize that many courses offered by two-year colleges can be transferred to four-year colleges and universities. Although this may not seem applicable for welding programs, you never know what changes the future may bring, and you may want to pursue additional college studies later. In that case, you will be a step ahead to have completed at least some courses which are transferrable such as English and other general studies courses. Courses offered by trade schools, on the other hand, are not generally considered college level and will not be accepted by four-year institutions.

Of course, if landing a job in welding is your single objective, a trade school may be a good choice. Still, many two-year colleges offer the same kind of programming as an option to their full-degree programs, allowing you to take welding courses without pursuing an associate degree and the general studies courses it requires. And in most cases, two-year college tuition is much less expensive than that charged by trade schools.

In choosing a school, make sure you understand just what type of school it represents. The name itself may not be a totally accurate indicator, for some trade schools refer to themselves as colleges but do not actually offer college-level work. Some others are called institutes, and in this case the school could qualify as a college or might be a trade school, depending on a number of factors.

Getting Accurate Information

Because different features are offered by different kinds of schools, you will want to know exactly where an institution fits in the overall scheme of things. To get an accurate picture, take a close look at a current catalog for any school in which you are interested. Look under ''degrees offered'' or ''programs offered'' and determine whether graduates earn diplomas, certificates, or associate (two-year) degrees. At the same time, read any descriptions of transfer programs, relationships with other institutions (such as membership in a state community college system), and other basic information about the school as a whole.

Next, look in the index and find the section on welding. Read the general program description, paying particular attention to such details as what kind of positions graduates are prepared to fill, level of program offering, length of time expected for completing a program, and similar details.

Also, take time to read the descriptions of welding courses, which may be found in a different section of the catalog (look under ''curriculum'' or ''course descriptions,'' usually located toward the back of the catalog). Such details may not be exciting or glamorous, but they will provide a good preliminary idea of the information you really need to make a good choice. Conversely, don't let photos of attractive students or other public relations gimmicks affect your review of this material. Colorful brochures and posters are fine, but their purpose is to make you feel good about the prospect of attending a given school, not to provide the detailed information you can find in catalog program descriptions.

COST FACTORS

In choosing any school that offers a welding program, a major factor to consider is the cost of attending. Tuition, fees, and other costs are rarely consistent from one school to the next. The cost of attending can range from nothing to thousands of dollars. Unless cost is not of importance to you, be sure to find out ahead just what expenses are involved in attending any program.

Schools Run by Public Agencies

Because they are supported by tax dollars, the schools with the lowest costs for tuition and related costs are those run by public agencies such as a public school system (including both regular and adult education courses) and programs funded by special grants such as the Job Training Partnership Act (described in more detail in chapter 5). In many cases, programs run by these agencies cost little or nothing to the individual student.

Public Two-Year Colleges

Next come public two-year colleges. Such institutions usually operate under an open admissions philosophy and try to keep their costs as low as possible so that virtually anyone can attend, regardless of financial status. Although amounts vary, a typical community, junior, or technical college will charge less than a thousand dollars for a full year of studies. Compared with the high cost of most universities and four-year colleges, this is quite inexpensive. At the same time, even this reasonably low amount can present problems for many students, but fortunately a variety of financial aid programs is available to students who need monetary assistance.

Private Schools

The most expensive option is provided by proprietary schools, privately owned trade schools, and private two-year colleges. These schools tend to cost substantially more because they do not qualify to receive state or local tax funds due to their private status. As a result, they must cover operating expenses with higher tuition and fees than those normally assessed by public institutions. At many privately run schools, it may take hundreds or even several thousand dollars to finish a short-term training program in a field such as welding. Unless you have a compelling reason to attend a privately funded school or college, it may be in your best interest to attend an institution that is supported by local or state taxes.

In some instances, of course, the option provided by a private school may still be best. If a public school within commuting distance does not offer a welding program, for example, it may be less costly to attend a nearby trade school than to attend a far-off college or school. Or if a particular trade school has an outstanding track record in training students and placing them in good jobs, it may be worth pursuing.

A balancing factor is that students who enroll at more costly schools tend to receive larger amounts of student aid. Since government financial aid programs base awards in part on the average cost of attending each institution, they usually make larger financial aid awards to students attending schools that charge high tuition. It is important to realize, though, that much of your financial aid package may come in the form of student loans, which must be repaid in the years following completion of your studies. So before agreeing to attend a relatively expensive school, make certain you understand the exact extent of financial obligations on your part, both up front and in the future.

REPUTATION AND RESULTS

Cost is only part of the equation for a successful educational experience. You also want to make certain that you receive high quality instruction. To get an idea of any school's quality, try to find out as much as possible about the school's past record of serving students in fields such as welding. Talk to people who might be in a position to comment on the school's effectiveness and reputation. For example, recent graduates can give you a firsthand assessment of just how well the school served their needs. Similarly, persons such as teachers, counselors, current students, and employers who hire graduates are good sources of information about a school or college.

School officials themselves are also a helpful source of information, but keep in mind that it is part of their job to make their institution sound attractive. This does not necessarily mean officials will be dishonest, but as a potential student, you need to think like a consumer who is about to make an important purchase. In considering any school, look at factors such as these.

Profit-making Intent

Does the school exist to make money? If so, it may operate differently than public institutions. The goal of making a profit may place more emphasis on business considerations than student needs.

Job Placement

Does the school operate a job placement office? Does it work closely with employers? What percentage of welding graduates find jobs in their field? In many cases this figure will be 90 percent or more. In any case, a strong placement service is a must unless you already have employment arranged.

Accreditation

Always check to see if the school is accredited. Holding a license or certificate of approval by the state is not the same as being accredited by a regional or national accrediting body. State licensing often means simply that a school has obtained permission to operate. Instead, see if the school lists accreditation by recognized bodies. For a community or technical college, watch for accreditation by a regional association such as the Southern Association of Colleges and Schools, the North Central Association of Colleges and Schools, the New England Association, or a similar organization. For a trade school, see if it is accredited by the National Association of Trade and Technical Schools. The latter is not on the same level of comprehensiveness as a regional accrediting agency for a college, but it is one positive indicator.

Ethical Practices

Unfortunately, all schools do not operate in an ethical manner. In looking at any school—particularly privately funded schools which exist to turn a profit—stay alert for efforts to grab students' money. Where there is money to be made, some dishonest people will surface. This happens in education as well as other fields, and every state has some schools that take advantage of unsuspecting students. The most common approach is to "help" the students obtain government grants and loans and then have this money paid to the school even though the students may not receive adequate instruction. In too many instances, schools have closed down, leaving students owing thousands of dollars in government or private loans. Or the schools continue to operate, but students do not receive adequate training and face difficulty in obtaining jobs.

Be alert for such practices. Recruiters for some schools may make everything sound easy and simple, basing their arguments on easy access to financial aid. If you feel doubts about a school, back off before signing anything and check around (with the local chamber of commerce, your school counselor, or the personnel office of a local company that employs welders) to see if it has achieved a reputation for following through on promises.

WEIGHING EDUCATIONAL OPTIONS

After you have gathered some basic information about one or more schools, take your time in deciding which represents the best choice. A too-hasty decision can be a mistake. This is especially likely if a recruiter for a school tries to rush you into signing admission forms or financial aid papers. The smart approach is to refuse to let yourself be hurried or pressured into enrolling.

Obtaining Information

In considering your choice, try to obtain as much information at possible. Read catalogs, brochures, and disclosure statements about financial policies. Take time to talk to friends, educational officials, or others whose advice you trust. Ask yourself, "If I were an employer, would I hire a graduate of this school's welding program?"

Visiting Campuses

Also, make sure you get a firsthand look at any school before enrolling rather than simply relying on written materials. In visiting the campus, make sure you get a feel for the school as a whole and not just the admissions office.

Take a look at classrooms, recreational facilities, the library, and the welding lab facilities. Consider whether the school seems to have up-to-date equipment and a pleasant learning environment.

If possible, find out how many students are enrolled in welding courses. That way, you can get an idea of the popularity and strength of the program. Bigger is not necessarily better, but a very small enrollment may indicate the program is floundering and subject to possible termination.

Pay attention to overall building condition and appearances. Often, schools of questionable quality will be located in facilities that are outdated and in many ways inadequate. On the other hand, appearances can be deceiving, so don't base your entire opinion of a school on its facilities. Talk to current students and see how they have fared to date and gather any other information that might be available. You can then make an informed decision instead of simply signing up for the first school you consider.

PAYING FOR EDUCATIONAL COSTS

If you attend a college or trade school, you will need to pay for the experience. Unlike high school, most such instruction will be available only after you have paid tuition and other costs.

The type and amount of costs involved vary not only from one state to the next but from one school to the next. Here are some of the costs that might be charged:

- Tuition—may be charged as a lump sum, per class or per credit hour, or some other way
- Application fees—sometimes required before enrollment
- Fees (general)—sometimes called just *fees* rather than tuition
- Lab fees—may be assessed to cover the cost of equipment and supplies for welding or other courses
- Student activity fees—often assessed even if you do not plan to take part in optional student activities
- Room and board—for students who do not commute to school, expenses for lodging and food represent a substantial investment
- Health fees—used to support student health services
- Book costs—seldom assessed along with tuition and fees, but you will normally be expected to buy all your own books
- Other fees—separate fees for taking special tests, having transcripts sent to employers or other schools, parking, and other purposes

Of course the greatest cost is basic tuition and fees. The largest portion of your educational dollars will go toward this basic charge.

Financial Aid Available

Although going to school may be expensive, students who need assistance can obtain financial support from a variety of sources. If you need help, you should be able to land a grant, scholarship, loan, or other award to help cover basic educational expenses.

Even though Congress has reduced the dollars available through some student aid programs and new restrictions have been imposed in some cases, the U.S. government still supports millions of students through a variety of aid programs. Most states also support their own programs for loans, grants, or other awards. And many private funding sources also provide aid. For students who take the time and trouble to apply for it, a wide range of financial assistance is available.

By supporting grants and loans for college, the federal government tries to ensure that everyone who needs help to pay for college has an opportunity to obtain hundreds or thousands of dollars in student aid. In the process, American students receive more than ten billion dollars in aid from the federal government yearly.

It is true that meeting the qualifications for federal aid can be difficult for families who are not significantly disadvantaged. In other words, the more income and assets your family has, the harder it will be to qualify for student aid. Yet even in situations where financial need is not as great, low interest loans and other forms of aid are frequently available.

Also, individual colleges and universities themselves provide a wide range of financial aid awards including scholarships, loans, and grants. In addition, thousands of private organizations sponsor special aid programs ranging from scholarships to grants.

For those students in welding and other fields who are aggressive in pursuing it, plenty of financial aid is available. If you want to attend a trade school, community college, or other institution, chances are excellent that you will be able to obtain the needed funds.

Qualifying for Federal Financial Aid

To obtain student aid provided or sponsored by the U.S. government, you must first complete a standard application which asks for information about your family's income, assets, debts, and other financial matters. This information is kept confidential, so don't be reluctant to provide such details. They are essential in any decisions that will be made about how much aid you can receive.

In most cases, one of the following forms needs to be completed to begin your financial aid request process:

- The U.S. Department of Education's Application for Federal Aid (AFSA)
- The American College Testing Program's Family Financial Statement (FFS)
- The College Scholarship Service's Financial Aid Form (FAF).
- The Student Aid Application for California (SAAC)
- The Illinois State Scholarship Commission's Application for Federal and State Student Aid (AFFSA)
- The Pennsylvania Higher Education Assistance Agency's Application for Pennsylvania State Grant and Federal Student Aid

The required forms can be obtained directly from the sponsoring agency, from high school guidance counselors, and from financial aid offices in colleges and proprietary schools. Check with a counselor if you are unsure which form is best for your situation.

Although the forms may seem imposing and some parents may be reluctant to divulge personal financial information, the trouble will be more than worth it. After all, just a few hours of effort in filling out forms can bring hundreds or thousands of dollars in grants, loans, work-study positions, or other student aid.

In applying for student aid, be sure to observe application deadlines closely. It is usually best to apply on or about January 1 of the calendar year in which you plan to begin studying in a community college, trade school, or other institution. In some cases, schools may ask you to apply even earlier. In any case, the sooner you apply, the better. For some programs, money is available on a first come, first-served basis, and in any event, you can make plans more effectively once you know your financial aid status. The deadline for most federally supported programs, if you delay applying, is normally the first business day in May.

Available Federal Aid Programs

Several different aid programs are sponsored by the federal government. Each program has its own advantages and eligibility criteria. When considering them, however, be sure to realize that many students receive awards from more than one program at the same time in a combined package.

Pell Grants

For those who have genuine financial need, perhaps the most desirable of all the government awards is a Pell Grant. These grants, which were previously called Basic Educational Opportunity Grants, or BEOGs, have helped millions of students pursue a postsecondary education. The great thing about a grant is that is represents a free investment in your future. Unlike loans, grants need not be repaid. You receive the award, use it to pay tuition or other costs, and go on from there without further obligation.

If you qualify for a Pell Grant, you can receive up to $2300 a year for educational expenses at the school of your choice. This amount will vary with each individual student. Whether you qualify (and if so, how much you will receive) depends not on grades or other factors but financial considerations such as number of children in the family, parents' income, debts, and assets. Another key factor is the cost of attending a given school, with Pell Grants generally being larger for students who attend more expensive schools.

The main thing to remember about these grants is that if you really need one, you will probably get it. The whole purpose of Pell Grants is to provide student aid to those with the greatest need. So the needier your family is, the better your chance of obtaining a large award.

About four to six weeks after completing your application for a Pell Grant, you will find out if you are eligible. This will be reported on a Student Aid Report (SAR), a form that you will receive in the mail. This information will also be used by officials at schools where you apply to determine if you receive awards through other government programs.

Supplemental Educational Opportunity Grants

A related program provides Supplemental Educational Opportunity Grants (SEOGs). Like Pell Grants, these awards do not have to be repaid, but while everyone who qualifies for a Pell Grant receives one, the number of SEOG awards available at each school is limited. As a result, even if you are eligible, you can miss out on an award under the SEOG program unless you apply early.

The amount of money available to individual students under this program is even higher than with Pell Grants. It is possible to receive as much as four thousand dollars a year through an SEOG award.

Loan Programs

If you don't qualify for a grant or need additional funds, another option is provided by various loans either offered by the federal government or made by other lending agencies with government backing.

PERKINS LOANS

One of the most useful of these is the Perkins Loans. Previously called National Direct Student Loans, they provide up to nine thousand dollars for four years of postsecondary study. Either combined with a grant or used as a single source of aid, these loans can furnish the necessary funds for tuition and related costs. An advantage is that interest rates are lower than normal bank loans, lessening the overall amount that must be repaid. Another plus is that payments may be stretched over a long period of time to make the financial burden less of a problem.

STAFFORD LOANS

Stafford Loans (previously known as Guaranteed Student Loans or GSLs) provide similar benefits. A difference is that the money is borrowed directly from a financial institution such as a savings and loan, bank, or credit union. Because the government backs the loans, lending agencies can offer lower interest rates than with many conventional loans, meaning the loans are more affordable.

For students who cannot demonstrate sufficient financial hardship but still need help, other loan programs are available. For example, almost anyone with a good credit rating can obtain PLUS loans or SLS loans (Supplement Loans for Students). PLUS loans are made to parents rather than students while with SLS loans just the opposite is true. In either case, the loans are made through banks or other private lenders.

Work-Study Program

Many students earn part of their educational costs by participating in the college work-study program. Here, students are placed in part-time jobs, usually at their college but sometimes with community agencies. For example, a work-study assignment might mean serving as a lab assistant, working in the college's library or bookstore, or helping out in an administrative office. Or it might mean participating in a special literacy program as a tutor or clerical assistant.

Students who work in this program earn at least the federal minimum wage. At the same time, they acquire valuable work experience and get to know college administrators and faculty members in a different way than other students. Often, new graduates find their job searches enhanced by positive recommendations obtained from their work-study supervisors.

Other Sources of Aid

In addition to government aid programs, stay alert for other types of financial aid. These can include:

- Scholarships and grants offered by schools themselves
- Special scholarships sponsored by organizations to which you or a parent belong (such as churches, civic clubs, lodges)
- Company scholarship programs (for example, the company where your father works may sponsor scholar-

ships for sons and daughters of employees). Or a local company that employs welders may have established a scholarship fund at your school or college
- Any other source of aid for which you may be eligible (look through college catalogs, financial aid brochures, and other sources of information to identify them)

GETTING ADMITTED

Applying for admission to a welding program should not be as complicated as competing for a spot in the freshman class at some prestigious liberal arts college. Nevertheless, certain procedures must be followed even to gain admission at a community college which operates under an open admissions policy.

Make sure you follow these steps when applying for a spot in a welding program:

Apply early. The earlier you apply, the less you have to worry about being turned away because a class has been filled or because some required paperwork is missing.

Provide all requested information. This may include filling out an admissions form, authorizing your high school to send a transcript of your academic record, and similar information.

Get tests out of the way. Many schools, especially colleges, require incoming students to take exams so they can be properly placed in the right classes. If you are asked to take placement tests or other exams, try to get them out of the way before the school year begins so you won't be held up during the busy period when classes are first starting.

Keep copies of written materials. Once you complete an application or other form, be sure to keep a photocopy. The same goes for test results or other paperwork. That way if anything is misplaced, you won't have to start over.

Be polite. In dealing with admissions officials, always be polite and cooperative. Applicants who are seen as pushy or uncooperative seldom have their applications placed at the top of anyone's list.

Follow up. If you have applied for admission but have not heard anything for several weeks, send a note or letter inquiring about your status. Then when you do receive a response, keep track of anything that is required on your part to follow up on the application.

TYPICAL COURSES

When you are considering a school or particular welding course, take a look at the descriptions provided in the school catalog. Or ask for sample course outlines, which are sometimes called syllabi (syllabus in the singular). Course descriptions provide basic information about the material to be covered, including prerequisites—courses and other requirements which must have been completed before enrolling.

Following are some representative course descriptions for welding courses offered by Greenville Technical College in Greenville, South Carolina.

Welding 102—Inert Gas Welding. A study of inert gas welding consisting of the study of equipment practices, different uses and advantages of this type of welding, and the general practice of inert gas welding.

Welding 113—Gas & Arc Welding. The study of the basic principles and practices of oxyacetylene welding and cutting and electric arc welding. Emphasis is placed on practice in fundamental position welding and safety procedures.

Welding 115—Arc & Acetylene Welding. An introduction to basic gas and arc welding as applied to the machinist in the repair and manufacture of tools and equipment with instruction in the gas and arc welding of small parts and tools.

Welding 117—Field Welding. The study of principles of oxyacetylene and arc welding. Application in the usage of portable welding equipment is also emphasized.

Welding 122—Properties, Testing, and Treatment of Metals. Covers methods of manufacturing steel, the modern blast furnace, cast iron, brass, stainless steel, and aluminum.

Welding 123—Arc Welding T & P. Covers the principles and practices of arc welding on ferrous and nonferrous metals with instruction in setting the correct machine settings, maintaining the proper care of machines and equipment, and using safe practices and procedures in different positions.

Welding 125—Automotive Welding. A study of principles of oxyacetylene and arc welding, basic principles of cutting, and applications of each as applied to auto repairs.

Welding 134—Shielded Metal Arc Pipe Welding. Covers the principles and practices of welding steel pipe, setting and adjusting machines, and safe procedures in different positions.

Welding 139—Testing Welded Joints. Covers both destructive and nondestructive testing of welded joints with instruction in conducting guided bend tests.

Welding 144—Burning, Fitting, & Welding Pipe Joints. Covers structural joint design and layout, the making and use of templates for pipe and tubing, pipe symbols, pipe code welding, and basic estimating procedures.

Welding 146—Advanced Welding Practices. A continuation of arc, gas, and inert welding with instruction in perfecting techniques on selected types of welding.

Welding 270—Specialized Welding. An introduction to welding procedures and practices in M.I.G. flux-core and sub-arc welding.

Welding 271—Specialized Welding II. A continuation of Welding 270 with instruction in perfecting techniques using T.I.G. processes on carbon steel pipe with carbon and stainless filler metals. Performance tests of all pipe procedures mastered will be given.

Most students do not take all these courses, but only those directly related to their program. Some courses are more advanced and cannot be taken until basic courses known as prerequisites have been completed. But a review of the total listing of welding courses offered by any school can be revealing.

Once you enroll in a welding course, it is best to obtain a course outline or syllabus. Many instructors distribute outlines of this type during the first class meeting. They vary in content and approach, but most will include objectives of the course, information about requirements such as textbooks or tools, how grades (if any) will be determined, and other important information.

Following is a typical outline for a welding course offered in a community college.

Course number: Welding 110

Course title: Gas and Arc Welding Fundamentals

Lecture hours per week: three
Lab/shop hours per week: nine
Total semester hours credit: six

Course description: This course provides the student with an overview of the basic fundamentals of gas welding (primarily oxyacetylene) and electric arc welding. Both theory and practice will be covered, with emphasis on basic position welding.

Textbook: *Welding Basics* by M.M. Smith

Required equipment: safety glasses, goggles, striker, pliers, gloves

Learning objectives:

1. To become familiar with basic oxyacetylene welding including flat butt and vertical welding, brazing, and cutting

2. To become familiar with basic arc welding including bead building and flat, vertical, and horizontal fillet welds

3. To master fundamental safety concepts and procedures

Grading scale:

   A   90–100
   B   80–89
   C   70–79
   D   60–69
   F   below 60

Grades will be based on two exams (40 percent of grade), demonstration of mastery through shop performance (50 percent), and attendance/participation (10 percent).

Topics to be covered weekly:

Week 1: Introduction to course (chapters 1 and 2)

Week 2: Basic safety procedures (chapter 3 plus handout 1)

Week 3: Overview of oxyfuel welding (chapter 4 and 5; handouts 2 and 3)

Weeks 4–5: Oxyfuel applications (chapters 6 and 7)

End of Week 6: Exam

Weeks 7–8: Pipe and plate welding (oxyacetylene)

Week 9: Overview of arc welding

Weeks 10–12: Arc welding applications

Weeks 13–14: Review and practice

Week 15: Final exam

Whenever you enroll in a course, make sure you obtain any outline or syllabus that is available. By consulting it frequently, you can keep the overall goals of the course clearly in mind as well as keeping close tabs on assignments and other requirements.

CHAPTER 5

SPECIAL TRAINING PROGRAMS

Welding programs offered by schools and colleges are not the only way to obtain training in the field. You can also learn the basics of welding through special programs such as apprenticeships, government-sponsored training programs, and employee training furnished by companies that employ welders.

APPRENTICESHIPS

(A traditional way to master a craft or trade is serving as an apprentice. Here, you learn basic techniques by working under the guidance of experienced workers.)

Apprenticeships in various crafts have provided career opportunities for centuries. During the Middle Ages, workers who wanted to learn a craft such as carpentry or glass making got their start by becoming apprentices. After serving for a specified number of years and demonstrating competency in the craft area, the apprentice would be admitted as a full-fledged member of a guild or similar organization.

In more recent times, the apprentice system has become less common, but it is still a legitimate training method used in many trades. In the case of welding, apprenticeships covering a broad range of metalworking may include the basics of welding. The International Association of Machinists and Aerospace Workers, for example, includes welding as a part of its basic apprenticeship program. The association lists the following responsibilities of apprentices (operating under the jurisdiction of a joint apprenticeship committee composed of members of the union, and the employer) in its *Apprenticeship Training Manual:*

1. To diligently and faithfully perform the work of the trade and to perform such other pertinent duties as may be assigned by the employer's supervisor of apprentices which are related to the apprentice's total training program.

2. To respect the property of the employer and abide by the rules and regulations of the employer, the union, and the committee.

3. To regularly attend and satisfactorily complete the required hours of related instruction as required under this apprenticeship program.

4. To maintain such records of work experience and training received on the job and in related instruction as may be required by the committee.

5. To develop safe working habits and conduct themsel-
    ves in their work in such a manner as to assure their
    own safety and that of their fellow workers.
6. To work for the employer to whom indentured by the
    completion of apprenticeship unless terminated by
    the committee. Not to seek employment with another
    employer within the jurisdictional area of this pro-
    gram without prior clearance of the committee, the
    union, and the employer to whom indentured.
7. To conduct themselves, at all times, in a creditable,
    ethical, and moral manner, trying to realize that
    much time, money, and effort will be spent in afford-
    ing the apprentice an opportunity to become a skilled
    journeyman.

Working as an apprentice is a time-honored tradition, one
that for centuries has provided a pathway for newcomers to
learn the intricacies of various crafts. It gives you the
opportunity to learn skills such as welding under the supervision of persons who have had years of experience in the
field.

COMPANY-SPONSORED PROGRAMS

In addition to apprenticeships, which are often run by
trade unions, some companies offer their own training
programs in welding. They range from formal programs
run much like those in schools to informal training situa-

tions where newcomers learn the ropes in a way much like apprenticeships but without strict requirements such as a specific number of hours that must be completed in training.

To find out about company-sponsored programs, check with the personnel office at a company that employs welders and ask if such programs are available. During times when additional welders are needed, newspaper ads may list details about such programs. In many cases, persons who already have experience in welding will be given preference in hiring, but in others, newcomers will be welcomed under the philosophy that the company can train its new workers in exactly the way it prefers and with the company's specific production needs kept paramount.

COMPANY START-UP TRAINING

In several states, special training is made available for new companies or those that have moved to a new location. In some cases, instruction is provided at no charge to the company or the individual worker, thus providing a great opportunity to break into the field.

In South Carolina, for example, the state's sixteen technical colleges and the State Board for Comprehensive and Technical Education offer a joint program known as ''Special Schools.'' Under this program, a company that relocates or begins anew in the state can receive free start-up training for its new employees. The state provides this as an incentive for industry to expand and thus bolster the state's economy while the company benefits by obtaining local workers who are trained promptly and effectively.

For the individual, such programs furnish a chance to get started and receive training without paying to go to school or waiting months or more to land a good job. Instead, persons who are hired to help start the company usually go through a rapid, intensive training program and begin earning good wages more quickly than through most other avenues.

If a company moved into a new area and needed large numbers of welders, a program such as this could provide training and job opportunities in welding for men and women who had not previously worked in the field. This would be less likely in general welding than in assembly-line work or similar operations, but it does represent an alternative training method in some locales.

MAKING THE MOST OF COMPANY AND APPRENTICESHIP TRAINING

If you find yourself participating in an apprenticeship or company-sponsored training program, try to observe these tips for a successful experience:

Be on time. You can make a bad impression from the very start by ignoring this basic consideration. And chronic problems with lateness can get you into real trouble. The simple solution: always make it a habit to go to work or classes a few minutes early, and you will not need to worry about this problem.

Ask questions. As you learn the basics of welding, be sure to ask questions as they arise. The degree to which you can do this will depend on the personality of senior personnel with whom you work, as some persons enjoy answering loads of questions while others become irritated with too many. You will need to adapt to your own work setting, but, in general, the more questions, the better.

Learn to handle criticism. In a learn-by-doing process, anyone is bound to make plenty of mistakes, especially at first. Don't become upset if your work is criticized—such analysis and comment is exactly what you need. Instead, learn from any criticism that comes your way.

Give it your best. Try hard, and those teaching and working with you will know it. Some people learn faster than others, and if you master things quickly, fine. But if not, keep trying and don't become discouraged. Redo or replace work as often as necessary or put in extra practice mastering specific welding techniques. If you give the learning process your best effort, positive results are much more likely. And the persons evaluating your progress will be more positive about your efforts than would otherwise be the case.

Show respect. In most cases, experienced welders will be older than you. Even if not, their knowledge deserves respect. When you are a student, in a way, everyone else is your boss (or at least is seen as a notch above you). Be sure to realize this and act respectfully in talking and dealing with others. You need not bow down or cater to anyone's inflated sense of self-importance, but try to be uniformly respectful and cooperative with instructors or fellow workers.

Follow the rules. Every corporate training program or apprenticeship has strict rules about what kind of learning opportunities you will receive as well as the limits on work you can perform at each stage of development. Be sure that you know what these rules are and that you follow them closely. Otherwise, you could miss out on key elements of instruction at best, and at worst, find yourself disciplined or even dropped from the program.

Look ahead. If an apprenticeship or training program seems too demanding, just think ahead and picture yourself working as an experienced welder, passing on tips to a newcomer to the field. Remember, any training program will end sooner or later, and the results will be worth all of your efforts.

MANPOWER TRAINING PROGRAMS

For several decades, the U.S. government has supported special training programs in welding and other fields designed to limit unemployment while helping meet the needs of employers for trained workers. Many state and local programs have provided such training through funding from the Manpower Development and Training Act (MDTA) in the 1960s, the Comprehensive Employment and Training Act (CETA) in the 1980s, and the Job Training Partnership Act (JTPA) in the 1980s and 1990s. This latter program supports a variety of training approaches, including providing funds for companies or schools to offer special training in fields for which workers are needed.

A difference in JTPA and previous programs is that more emphasis is placed on partnerships between employers and educational institutions. This is beneficial to students because emphasis is placed not just on training, but on placing students in jobs after initial training has been completed.

Another plus is that JTPA programs can be offered by a variety of organizations, not just schools. For example, in many cities, groups such as the Urban League sponsor JTPA training. Private companies with a need for more welders can also obtain funds through JTPA channels to hold special, short-term training programs.

Because JTPA programs are designed to make people employable who might not otherwise obtain or hold down good jobs, they have special admissions standards based on income, unemployment, or other factors. To find out more, contact the JTPA Private Industrial Council in your community.

CHAPTER 6

ORGANIZATIONS AND CERTIFICATIONS

Welders seldom work in isolation. Persons employed in the field not only work side by side with other welders but also participate in organizations related to their professional interests. These groups include labor unions, professional societies, and other organizations.

In addition, welders frequently undergo a certification process designed to assure that their work meets specific standards. Some welders hold several different types of certifications while others specialize in a single type of welding and thus deal with only one type of certification process.

LABOR UNIONS

Many welders and those holding related positions belong to labor unions. Unions, which are organizations in which workers band together to promote the welfare of members of the group in relations with employers, have been an integral part of American business and industry since the 1880s. Many advancements such as shorter workweeks, higher pay, fringe benefits, and workers' rights have been initiated by labor unions.

Persons employed in welding and related occupations belong to a number of unions, according to the U.S. Department of Labor. These include:

- International Association of Machinists and Aerospace Workers
- International Brotherhood of Boilermakers, Iron Ship Builders, Blacksmiths, Forgers and Helpers
- International Union, United Automobile, Aerospace and Agricultural Implement Workers of America
- United Association of Journeymen and Apprentices of the Plumbing and Pipe Fitting Industry of the United States and Canada
- United Electrical, Radio, and Machine Workers of America

As an example of the benefits and responsibilities offered by a labor union, consider the International Association of Machinists and Aerospace Workers (IAM). Workers in this union do not receive separate training as welders if they undergo apprentice training but instead cover it along with other content studied during the apprenticeship. At any rate, members benefit from a long-standing, highly successful union track record. Formed over one hundred years ago, the union now has over 800,000 members in North

America, Puerto Rico, and Panama. Its members work in a wide range of industries and hold many different kinds of jobs.

According to the union's publication "Profile of a Trade Union," the IAM guarantees all members the following rights:

- The right to membership in the union regardless of race, sex, or national origin
- The right to attend union meetings (and to speak freely)
- The right to nominate members for offices in the organization
- The right to vote for members for offices in the union, to vote on proposals regarding negotiations with management, and to speak out freely against policies or candidates for union office
- The right to run for union offices
- The right to vote by secret ballot regarding any strike action
- The right to receive strike benefits (after being a member three months)
- The right to receive an accounting of union finances and to be informed on union policy
- The right to propose changes in the union's constitution and to elect local delegates to conventions where votes are taken on such changes

Like other unions, the IAM is financed by dues from members. The minimum amount paid by any member is the equivalent of two hours' wages per month. In return for money paid into the organization, members receive not only the rights listed above but also benefit from the union's ongoing efforts to attain better wages, working conditions, and employee rights for its members.

For instance, the union uses collective bargaining to seek cost-of-living wage increases, paid sick leave and medical benefits, joint apprenticeship and retraining on the job, pension benefits, safe working conditions, and other benefits and improvements.

The union also works to influence legislation on behalf of its members. It encourages tax reform, enforcement of government safety regulations, and other matters related to the well-being of members of the union.

Unions are stronger and more predominant in some locations than in others. In the industrialized Northeast, for example, labor unions are commonplace. In southern states such as South Carolina, Georgia, and Alabama, on the other hand, unions have never grown to be as strong or as common.

In addition to geographical considerations, union membership may be affected by other factors such as size. Some smaller companies may not be unionized even when large firms in the same area are what is known as union shops. In any event, welders who belong to unions often find the benefits worth far more than the cost of union dues.

WELDING SOCIETIES

Persons interested in welding—whether or not they belong to unions— also may hold membership or otherwise be involved in professional societies designed to advance the welding field. Or they may participate in other related organizations.

The most widely known such organization is the American Welding Society. Headquartered in Miami, Florida, this organization has over thirty thousand members. It provides a number of services including the following:

- Sponsors conferences and seminars about welding
- Supports research in welding-related subjects
- Monitors technical advances and communicates them to members and other interested parties
- Provides information and technical data
- Publishes the highly respected periodical *Welding Journal*
- Publishes *Welding Handbook* and other publications
- Serves as a resource organization about issues and standards related to welding.

For more information about the society or any of its services, write to:

The American Welding Society
P.O. Box 351040
Miami, FL 33135

Several other welding organizations, while not as widely based in membership, advance the field through research or provide information of use to persons working in the field. These include:

The American Welding Institute
The Edison Welding Institute
The Welding Research Council

In addition, other organizations prove useful to meeting specific needs. Those who become teachers of welding, for example, may find it beneficial to participate in the American Vocational Association or statewide groups of vocational educators.

CERTIFICATIONS

Even after graduating from an appropriate welding training program, you will need to demonstrate that the work you perform meets certain standards. After all, the quality of work performed by welders is an important factor not only in employer satisfaction but in the safety of property and people. A commercial airliner carrying two hundred passengers, a supertanker full of oil, or a thirty-story building full of office workers, for example, all operate on the assumption that welders and others who constructed them did a good, solid job in the process.

To help guarantee the safety of these and other structures, government agencies and private employers may require welders to pass examinations to demonstrate competence in the type of welding to be performed. Although the process of taking such an exam may sound imposing at first, it actually is quite helpful to the individual as well as the company or agency conducting the testing. Advantages of the certification process include:

- Safety is assured for all those concerned
- Individual welders learn and improve their capabilities both from preparing for exams and the exam process itself
- Self-confidence is bolstered through successful completion of certification exams

Succeeding with Certification and Other Exams

If you need to take an exam for degree completion, certification, civil service qualifications, or other purposes, make certain to give the process its due while at the same time keeping from becoming unduly nervous about the prospect. After all, welders successfully make it through such experiences all the time.

To do the best possible job, though, you will need to follow measures such as the following:

- If there are written questions, read through all of them very quickly and then go back and start marking answers. That way you have a sense of the overall thrust of the questions. At the same time, your mind can begin attacking more than one question at the same time, at least on a subconscious basis. (Note: certification may rest entirely on an inspection of actual welding work, but written questions may be required in other circumstances).

- If there are time limits, make sure you are aware of them and that you keep track of time. Do not spend too much time on a minor task or section. Also, be sure to bring a watch; a clock may not be available, or it may not be functioning accurately.
- Practice ahead of time. If you will be required to demonstrate certain types of welds and then have them inspected, be sure you have spent plenty of time actually performing that type of welding task. The more practice time you spend, the better your work will be. And your level of confidence will be boosted.
- At least several days in advance, talk with a friend, instructor, or co-worker who has recently undergone the same process and obtain his or her insights about the experience. This can be especially helpful for inexperienced welders.
- Don't hesitate to pose questions to the examiner, if that individual is available. This does not mean asking for help, but be sure to ask any questions you might have about the exam or certification procedure.
- Don't be nervous. This is easier to say than to do, of course, but try to develop coping strategies. For example, use deep breathing to calm yourself just before the testing experience. Or keep in mind that the future of the civilized world does not depend on your results.

- Learn from mistakes. When you make mistakes, remember that everyone else makes mistakes, too. Instead of becoming discouraged, try to learn from any errors and apply that knowledge to future efforts.

Also, be sure to keep records regarding certifications and related matters. In some instances, you may be asked to demonstrate evidence of having successfully passed previous exams.

Welding can be a smart career choice for women since many employers are actively looking for female job applicants, and the pay is more attractive than for many other jobs. [Mountain View College (DCCD) photo]

CHAPTER 7

EARNINGS AND BENEFITS

EARNINGS

Persons employed in welding earn excellent wages and benefits. The American Welding Society (AWS) has studied wages for welding personnel around the country and consequently has made the following estimates:

> For persons trained to perform welding jobs, starting wages across the country range, on the average, from *three to five times* the minimum wage as established by the federal government. The actual amount varies with skill levels, location and other factors.*

Taking AWS estimates and applying them to the current minimum wage ($3.65 per hour), the following wage ranges can be projected.

---

*In some cases, these wages can be as much as *ten times* the minimum wage.

At the lower end of the scale (three times the minimum wage), a welder might earn something like this:

$10.95 per hour
$438 per week (40 hours)
$22,776 per year

At five times the minimum wage, earnings would be as follows:

$18.25 per hour
$730 per week
$37,413 per year

At up to ten times the minimum wage, the figures are even more impressive. In general, however, wage ranges for welders tend to be more meaningful than average wages since figures on which averages are based change frequently and wages can be affected by various factors. Factors that can influence wages include the following:

Location—Workers in urban areas tend to earn more than those in rural areas, for example.

Local cost of living—Wages can be influenced greatly by the local cost of living. In Alaska, for instance, a loaf of bread or a month's rent may cost more than twice the amount for an equivalent item in North Carolina or Kansas. As a result, wages must be higher to compensate for such differences.

National inflation—As inflation occurs at the national level, wages tend to increase—although not uniformly—across the country.

Skill levels—Highly complex welding jobs often pay higher wages than those requiring more basic skills. Similarly, individuals who can demonstrate superior skills can sometimes command higher wages than would otherwise be the case.

Local competition—The competition (or lack of it) with other firms employing welders can influence wages. If one company raises its wages, others may be forced to follow suit to avoid losing workers. Conversely, if only one organization has a need for welders, it may be able to offer somewhat lower wages.

Company business conditions—An aerospace company that has just landed a huge government contract may be in a position to offer attractive wages. An airline that has lost millions of dollars may find it necessary to cut wages. The financial health of a company can play a major factor in ability to pay high wages.

Longevity of company—New companies may pay less than more established firms. With less in the way of basic resources than more established companies, they may offer a chance to grow with the organization as partially offsetting lower pay.

FRINGE BENEFITS

In addition to wages, most employers pay a variety of fringe benefits to their employees. These are usually much more extensive for full-time employees than for part-time staff, and benefits vary from one company to another and in union and nonunion environments.

Typical benefits earned by welders include:

- Retirement or pension funds
- Medical insurance
- Paid vacation time
- Paid sick leave
- Workmen's compensation in case of injury
- Social security benefits

In addition, welders in some companies participate in profit-sharing programs, expanded medical coverage such as dental insurance or optical insurance, membership in credit unions, and other benefits that may vary widely from one employer to the next.

CHAPTER 8

OPPORTUNITIES FOR EVERYONE

As with other technical fields, welding has traditionally been dominated by white males. However, as society and the workplace have changed over the past two or three decades, the diversity of opportunities in this field has expanded significantly. Careers in welding today are open to individuals with a wide variety of backgrounds, and anyone who is interested in pursuing a welding career should be able to follow up on that desire.

WOMEN IN WELDING

Although most welders are still men, increasing numbers of women are beginning to enter this field. And their success is opening doors for more women welders in the future.

During World War II, many American factories relied on the work of female welders to take the place of men who were serving in the armed services. Women proved to be excellent workers in welding and other crafts involved in the construction of airplanes, tanks, ships, and other military equipment, along with normal welding functions needed outside the war effort.

Unfortunately, this turned out to be a temporary situation, for when the war ended in 1945, millions of men returned to civilian life and took back most of the jobs in industry. Recent years have seen women developing a new interest in welding careers, however, and more females have begun to enroll in welding programs and take jobs in the field.

Some reasons welding can be a smart career choice for women include:

- The pay is more attractive than for many other jobs.
- Many employers will give preference to female job applicants because few have traditionally held welding positions, and companies want to establish better track records in affirmative action guidelines and other contemporary policies.
- Female students can sometimes qualify for special financial aid and support programs, making school or college attendance less expensive or even free. For example, many schools offer programs supported by federal funds for gender equity and services for single parents and homemakers. These programs can furnish women with counseling services and in some cases pay for tuition, books, supplies, and even transportation and child care.

- Changing attitudes in the workplace and society as a whole have made it less unusual to find women working in technical fields such as welding.
- Women have already proven themselves as highly efficient welders, and any ideas that men are somehow "better" or ideally suited for welding jobs simply represent outdated thinking.

Of course, as with many technical fields, the majority of workers in welding in the immediate future will probably still be males. But the field is definitely open to women, and more and more female welders can be expected in years ahead.

OPPORTUNITIES FOR THE HANDICAPPED

Persons with handicaps or disabilities may be able to pursue careers in welding or a related area. As with any other technical career, the range of opportunities varies tremendously, depending on the type of disability or handicap, the degree to which it is restrictive, and specific job requirements. An individual confined to a wheelchair may not be able to perform some types of welding jobs, for example, but may be well suited for operating a specific type of welding machine. Or a person with a learning disability may be able to overcome barriers to learning and master the use of welding equipment.

(Many schools and colleges offer special programs to help handicapped students complete educational requirements and prepare for careers in various areas, including technical fields such as welding.) At New River Community College in Dublin, Virginia, special services are provided for students with hearing impairments. This includes interpreting of classroom lectures and other sessions from spoken language into sign language, the assistance of volunteer notetakers who take notes that help hearing-impaired students keep up with the rapid pace of college-level work, and special counseling and support services. A similar program provides extra help for students with learning disabilities. Such services are not available at all schools and colleges, but they are becoming increasingly common. For handicapped persons who feel a welding-related career represents a realistic possibility, special programs can make the difference in breaking into the field.

The IAM Cares program, sponsored by the International Association of Machinists and Aerospace Workers, is another example of efforts to enhance career possibilities for the handicapped. This program includes the following components:

- A Projects with Industry program, which helps disabled persons find and keep jobs
- The Transitional Services for Handicapped Youths program, which helps young people negotiate the change from an educational environment to the world of work

- A special jobs program that helps persons receiving social security disability benefits find jobs that they can perform
- A program operated in conjunction with the Department of Labor targeted to persons with disabilities.

These programs provide a variety of services including assessment, vocational guidance, job training, industrial evaluation, and job placement. Although many participants are members of the IAMAW or other unions, the program is also open to nonunion members.

In addition to special programs such as these, many other programs are available to assist handicapped persons. Vocational rehabilitation centers are located in every state, for example, where they provide a range of educational and placement services. Through these and other avenues, men and women with different handicapping conditions may explore career possibilities and, where appropriate, pursue positions as welders or workers in related areas.

OPPORTUNITIES FOR MINORITIES

Educational and career opportunities for members of minority groups are more wide ranging than ever before, and this is true in welding as in other areas of American society. Not only do federal laws protect individual rights in vital areas such as education and employment but many companies make concerted efforts to hire minorities. As they strive to meet company or government guidelines for affirmative action and equal opportunity, employers provide an open door for minority job applicants.

In addition, many special scholarships and academic support programs are available to minority students. Almost every school or college has financial aid or special support programs that provide students from minority groups with assistance in obtaining the training and credentials needed to qualify for good jobs.

BASIC REQUIREMENTS

Regardless of gender, race, or other considerations, persons planning to pursue a career in welding should possess certain traits. In its brochure on welding and joining, the American Welding Society lists these success factors for a career in welding:

1. Good mechanical ability: Do you understand how and why things work as they do?
2. Logical mind: Do you use common sense?
3. Learning skills: Have you acquired a basic knowledge of applied mathematics, materials, and drafting...and do you stay up to date?
4. A team player: Do you enjoy working with others? Are you willing to learn from co-workers and able to work under pressure?

5. Imagination: Are you creative and able to visualize a completed project while creating it from a plan?
6. Good physical condition: Have you stayed in good shape? Are you good with your hands, with strong manual coordination and good (correctable) eyesight?
7. Self-discipline and patience: Do you have what it takes to see a job through to completion?
8. A sense of integrity and responsibility: Do you respect the safety and lives of yourself, co-workers, and others? (Welding and joining affect the lives of thousands, perhaps millions, of people).

Certainly some factors may be offset by other considerations (for example, the ''good physical condition'' mentioned in item 6 would not apply in the same sense to a handicapped and a nonhandicapped person). But anyone seriously considering a career in welding should be able to respond positively to questions such as these.

Colleges and trade schools provide valuable training for welders. (Photo courtesy of Bessemer State Technical College)

CHAPTER 9

WHERE TO GO FROM HERE

If a welding career seems challenging now that you have reviewed the material provided in previous chapters, the next step is to chart a path for further development. Such a path will depend on your own particular background as well as future goals, but steps in this process might include any or all of the following:

- Checking what kinds of training programs are available to you
- Completing welding studies at the high school level
- Applying for admission to a two-year college or to a trade school
- Applying for financial aid
- Completing a diploma or degree program in welding
- Visiting companies where welders are employed to gain a feel for the work involved
- Completing a company-based training program or one sponsored by the government

- Landing a part-time job as a laborer or helper to gain exposure to welding
- Talking with counselors about prospects for a welding career
- Taking career interest tests or inventories to help establish your interest or potential for this kind of career

FINDING A JOB

Once you finish your education and are ready to work as a welder, you will need to take steps to find employment. Sometimes finding a job is as much a matter of luck and timing as anything else, and in some cases it may require very little effort. In other instances, you may have to work hard to land that first job. Whatever the case, you will need to know where to locate information about welding positions and how to follow up on that information.

Identifying Job Openings

The classified section of any newspaper continues to be one of the best ways to find out about job openings in welding. Here is a typical newspaper ad for positions in welding which appeared in the Atlanta *Journal and Constitution*:

Welders
Leading manufacturer of railroad freight cars has immediate openings for Production Welders. Applicants

should have a least 1 year of experience in MIG welding. Experience in flux core wire helpful.

Starting pay is $8.59/hour plus a 20% incentive bonus. All applicants are required to take a weld test. Position includes a fully company paid benefits program including pension, life insurance, medical and dental.

Ads are also found in magazines related to welding. A recent edition of *Welding Journal* listed these openings in its classified section:

- An ad seeking welding instructors placed by a community college (requirements included a bachelor's degree or a two-year degree and progress toward a bachelor's, plus five years of related work experience)
- An ad for a manufacturer's representative, where successful applicants would sell arc and resistance welding machines and systems
- An ad for a service technician to work on machine controls for plasma arc and oxy-fuel cutting machines

Many companies post job announcements on bulletin boards in addition to (or in place of) newspaper advertising. The personnel office will also have such information.

Your local employment service or job service office (provided by state or local government as a free service) also receives listings of job openings.

The placement office of a college or trade school is another place where you can find out about available jobs. Most schools operate such offices with the specific purpose of finding jobs for their students and graduates.

LANDING A JOB

Once you identify a job opening, you will probably have to fill out a job application. If an application is required, be sure to take your time in filling it out. Answer all questions completely and honestly. Be as neat as possible, and doublecheck spelling and grammar.

A completed application may be followed by a job interview. Whenever you are asked to come for an interview, be sure to take the following steps.

Plan ahead. Before the interview takes place, plan ahead for the experience. Try to anticipate possible questions and practice answering them. Also, try to obtain some basic information about the employer such as number of employees and products manufactured. That way, you will be better prepared to ask intelligent questions.

Dress neatly. Even though a welder's position does not require wearing dress clothes, don't make the mistake of showing up for an interview looking sloppy. The old truism about first impressions still has a lot of validity. Make certain you wear clean, neat clothes and are well groomed in terms of hairstyle and overall cleanliness before going on any interview, no matter how informal.

Show up on time. Always be punctual for an interview. Failure to show up on time may make an employer wonder if you will have a problem reporting to work on time.

Stay calm. Although interviews can be imposing, try to stay calm. Remember that even though you may have high hopes about a certain job, it will not be the end of the world if you are not hired. After all, there will be other interviews and other jobs. When you realize this, staying calm can be an easier task than might otherwise be the case.

Once you do land that first job, you will be on your way. Your career in welding will have begun, and you will have joined the ranks of a truly important occupation.

APPENDIX A

BIBLIOGRAPHY

Althouse, A.D., C.H. Turnquist, and W.A. Bowditch. *Modern Welding*. South Holland, Ill.: Goodheart-Willcox Publishers, 1980.

American Welding Society. "Welding and Joining."

International Association of Machinists and Aerospace Workers. "Apprenticeship and Policy Manual."

_____."Profile of a Trade Union."

National Association of Trade and Technical Schools. *Handbook*. 1989.

Sacks, Raymond J. *Essentials of Welding*. Peoria, Ill.: Bennett Publishing, 1984.

Schell, Frank R. and Bill Matlock. *Industrial Welding Procedures*. New York: Van Nostrand Reinhold, 1979.

U.S. Department of Labor. *Dictionary of Occupational Titles*. 1987.

Occupational Outlook Handbook. Lincolnwood, Ill.: VGM Career Horizons, 1990.

SCHOOLS OFFERING WELDING PROGRAMS

Private Trade and Technical Schools

The following private trade and technical schools are among those accredited by the National Association of Trade and Technical Schools (NATTS) to offer instructional programs in welding.

Arizona

ABC Technical and Trade
    Schools
    3761 East Technical Drive
    Tucson, AZ 85713
    (602) 748-1762

ABC Welding School
    2103 East Buckeye Road
    Phoenix, AZ 85034
    (602) 244-0387

Phoenix Technical and Trade
    School
    603 South First Avenue
    Phoenix, AZ 85003
    (602) 252-7304

California

American Technical Institute
    4600 Ashe Street
    Bakersfield, CA 93313
    (805) 835-9225

Consolidated Welding Schools
4343 Imperial Highway East
Lynwood, CA 90262
(213) 638-0418

Eduplex Career Center, Division
of Certified Welding and
Trade School
1028 East Compton
Boulevard
Compton, CA 90221
(213) 537-3824

Golden State School
2491 West Shaw Avenue
Fresno, CA 93703
(209) 224-5848

Long Beach Technical Institute
189 West Victoria Street
North Long Beach, CA
90805
(213) 604-8514

Pacific Coast Technical
Institute
1476 Island Avenue
San Diego, CA 92101
(619) 233-0133

Welding Trade School
765 Coleman Avenue
San Jose, CA 95110
(408) 297-3150

Colorado

International Technical Institute
Division of Certified
Welding
3701 South Kalamath
Englewood, CO 80110
(303) 781-7845

Connecticut

Hartford Modern School of
Welding
184 Ledyard Street
Hartford, CT 06114
(203) 249-7576

Technical Careers Institute
11 Kimberly Avenue
West Haven, CT 06516
(203) 932-2282

Florida

Apex Technical School
3501 Northwest Ninth
Avenue
Oakland Park, FL 33309
(305) 563-5899

Illinois

National Technical Schools
1201 West Adams
Chicago, IL 60607
(312) 666-5590

Kansas

United Technical Institute
　2015 South Meridian
　Wichita, KS 67213
　(316) 942-7733

Louisiana

Bayou Technical Institute
　P.O. Box 13128
　New Orleans, LA 70185

Maryland

Maryland Institute of
　　Technology
　121 Kane Street
　Baltimore, MD 21224
　(301) 633-4300

National Technical Institute
　4703 Decatur Street
　Edmondston, MD 20910
　(301) 277-2286

Michigan

Advanced Career Training
　　Division, Photon School
　　of Welding
　300 Ames Street
　Saginaw, MI 48602
　(517) 791-1644

Weldor Training Center
　520 West Eight Mile Road
　Ferndale, MI 48220
　(313) 399-3388

Minnesota

Dunwoody Industrial Institute
　818 Wayzata Boulevard
　Minneapolis, MN
　　55403-1192
　(612) 374-5800

Missouri

Ranken Technical Institute
　4431 Finney Avenue
　St. Louis, MO 63113
　(314) 371-0236

Sullivan Educational Centers
　1001 Harrison
　Kansas City, MO 64106
　(816) 471-1811

Vatterott Educational Centers
　3854 Washington Avenue
　St. Louis, MO 63108
　(314) 534-2586

New Jersey

General Technical Institute
　1118 Baltimore Avenue
　Linden, NJ 07036
　(201) 486-9353

Kalix Trade School
   7015 Westfield Avenue
   Pennsauken, NJ 08110
   (609) 663-6313

New York

Apex Technical School
   635 Avenue of the Americas
   New York, NY 10011
   (212) 924-7373

Modern Welding School
   1740 Broadway
   Schenectady, NY 12306
   (518) 374-1216

National Technical Schools
   476 Louisiana Street
   Buffalo, NY 14204
   (716) 842-6420

Ohio

Great Lakes Technical Institute
   1361 East Fifty-fifth Street
   Cleveland, OH 44103
   (216) 431-1050

Hobart School of Welding
      Technology
   Trade Square East
   Troy, OH 45373
   (513) 332-5215

Oklahoma

AAA Welding School
   9363 East Forty-sixth Street
      South
   Tulsa, OK 74145
   (918) 627-2699

Tulsa Welding School
   3038 Southwest Boulevard
   Tulsa, OK 74107

United Technical Institute
   4233 Charter Avenue
   Oklahoma City, OK 73108
   (405) 942-7700

Pennsylvania

Johnson Technical Institute
   3427 North Main Avenue
   Scranton, PA 18508
   (717) 342-6204

Kalix Trade School
   439 North Eleventh Street
   Philadelphia, PA 19123
   (215) 765-7208

National Technical Schools
   4725 Chestnut Street
   Philadelphia, PA 19139
   (215) 748-6101

New Castle School of Trades
   R.D. No. 1, Route 422
   Pulaski, PA 16143
   (412) 964-8811

Technician Training School
1000 Island Avenue
McKees Rocks, PA 15136
(412) 771-7590

Triangle Tech
P.O. Box 551
DuBois, PA 15801
(814) 371-2090

Washington Institute of
Technology
82 South Main Street
Washington, PA 15301
(412) 222-1942

Welder Training and Testing
Institute
230 Johnson Street
Wilkes Barre, PA 18702
(717) 823-0109

Williamson Free School of
Mechanical Trades
106 South New Middleton
Road
Media, PA 19063
(215) 566-1776

Tennessee

United Technical Institute
430 Allied Drive
Nashville, TN 37211
(615) 834-7451

Texas

American Traders Institute
2608 Hawes
Dallas, TX 75235
(214) 352-2222

Capitol City Trade & Tech
School
205 East Riverside Drive
Austin, TX 78704
(512) 444-3257

Simdex Technical Institute
8110 LaPorte Road
Houston, TX 77012
(713) 923-1110

Texas Vocational School
1913 South Flores
San Antonio, TX 78204
(512) 225-3253

Western Technical Institute
1000 Texas Avenue
P.O. Box M
El Paso, TX 79951
(915) 523-3737

Wyoming

Certified Welding & Trade
School
7030 Salt Creek Route, Box 7
Casper, WY 82601
(307) 266-2066

COLLEGES OFFERING WELDING PROGRAMS

In addition to trade schools, many two-year colleges offer welding programs. Over thirteen hundred junior, community, and technical colleges operate in the United States today. All of these institutions do not offer welding programs, but many do. To find out if a given two-year college teaches welding, simply consult its catalog or call the admissions office.

Or send a postcard to the central office for two-year colleges in any state in which you are interested and ask for a list of colleges that offer welding programs.

A partial listing of colleges offering welding programs follows. If your local community college is not listed, that does not necessarily mean that it does not offer welding, as this list is not all-inclusive but is offered only as representative information. For any college in which you are interested, contact the admissions office to make sure.

Alabama

George C. Wallace State
    Community College
Selma, AL 36701

George C. Wallace State
    Community College
Dothan, AL 36303

John C. Calhoun State
    Community College
Decatur, AL 35602

Northwest Alabama Junior
    College
Phil Campbell, AL 35581

Shelton State Community
    College
Tuscaloosa, AL 35404

Alaska

Islands College
    Sitka, AK 99835

Ketchican College
    Ketchikan, AK 99901

Arizona

Arizona Western College
    Yuma, AZ 85364

Central Arizona College
    Coolodge, AZ 85228

Cochise College
  Douglas, AZ 85607

Eastern Arizona College
  Thatcher, AZ 85552

Pima Community College
  Tucson, AZ 85709

Yavapai College
  Prescott, AZ 86301

California

American River College
  Sacramento, CA 95841

Bakersfield College
  Bakersfield, CA 93305

Cerritos College
  Norwalk, CA 90650

Chabot College
  Hayward, CA 94545

College of the Redwoods
  Eureka, CA 95501

Compton Community College
  Compton, CA 90221

De Anza College
  Cupertino, CA 95014

Fresno City College
  Fresno, CA 93741

Kings River Community
  College
  Reedley, CA 93654

Los Angeles Trade and
  Technical College
  Los Angeles, CA 90015

Orange Coast College
  Costa Mesa, CA 92626

Rio Hondo College
  Whittier, CA 90608

San Diego City College
  San Diego, CA 92101

Yuba College
  Marysville, CA 95901

Colorado

Aims Community College
  Greeley, CO 80631

Community College of Denver
  Denver, CO 80218

Front Range Community
  College
  Westminster, CO 80030

Pikes Peak Community College
  Colorado Springs, CO 80906

Pueblo Community College
  Pueblo, CO 81004

Trinidad State Junior College
  Trinidad, CO 81082

Delaware

Delaware Technical and
    Community College
Southern Campus
Georgetown, DE 19947

Florida

Brevard Community College
    Cocoa, FL 32922

Central Florida Community
    College
Oscala, FL 32670

Chipola Junior College
    Marianna, FL 32446

Indian River Community
    College
Fort Pierce, FL 33450

Okaloosa-Walton Junior
    College
Niceville, FL 32578

Santa Fe Community College
    Gainesville, FL 32601

Seminole Community College
    Sanford, FL 32771

South Florida Community
    College
Avon Park, FL 33825

Georgia

Bainbridge Junior College
    Bainbridge, GA 31717

Brunswick Junior College
    Brunswick, GA 31523

Dalton College
    Dalton, GA 30720

Dekalb College
    Decatur, GA 30034

Hawaii

University of Hawaii–Honolulu
    Community College
Honolulu, HI 96817

University of Hawaii–Kauai
    Community College
Lihue, HI 96766

University of Hawaii–Maui
    Community College
Kahului, HI 96732

Idaho

College of Southern Idaho
    Twin Falls, ID 83301

North Idaho College
    Coeur D'Alene, ID 83814

Ricks College
    Rexburg, ID 83440

Illinois

Belleville Area College
  Belleville, IL 62221

College of DuPage
  Glen Ellyn, IL 60137

Danville Area Community
  College
  Danville, IL 61832

Elgin Community College
  Elgin, IL 60120

Highland Community College
  Freeport, IL 61032

John A. Logan College
  Carterville, IL 62918

John Wood Community
  College
  Quincy, IL 62301

Joliet Junior College
  Joliet, IL 60436

Lewis and Clark Community
  College
  Godfrey, IL 62035

Lincoln Land Community
  College
  Springfield, IL 62708

Moraine Valley Community
  College
  Palos Hills, IL 60465

Oakton Community College
  Des Plaines, IL 60016

Rock Valley College
  Rockford, IL 61101

Triton College
  River Grove, IL 60171

Waubonsee Community
  College
  Sugar Grove, IL 60554

Indiana

Indiana Vocational Technical
  College–Central Indiana
  Indianapolis, IN 46202

Indiana Vocational Technical
  College–Kokomo
  Kokomo, IN 46901

Indiana Vocational Technical
  College–Lafayette
  Lafayette, IN 47905

Indiana Vocational Technical
  College–Northeast
  Fort Wayne, IN 46805

Indiana Vocational Technical
  College–Southwest
  Evansville, IN 47710

Indiana Vocational Technical
  College–Wabash Valley
  Terre Haute, IN 47802

Iowa

Des Moines Area Community
College
Ankeny, IA 50021

Iowa Central Community
College
Fort Dodge, IA 50501

Iowa Western Community
College
Council Bluffs, IA 51501

Kirkwood Community College
Cedar Rapids, IA 52406

North Iowa Community
College
Mason City, IA 50401

Kansas

Barton County Community
College
Great Bend, KS 67530

Butler County Community
College
El Dorado, KS 67042

Central College
McPherson, KS 67460

Coffeyville Community
College
Coffeyville, KS 67337

Colby Community College
Colby, KS 67701

Cowley County Community
College
Arkansas City, KS 67005

Dodge City Community
College
Dodge City, KS 67801

Fort Scott Community College
Fort Scott, KS 66701

Garden City Community
College
Garden City, KS 67846

Haskell Indian Junior College
Lawrence, KS 66044

Hutchinson Community
College
Hutchinson, KS 67501

Independence Community
College
Independence, KS 67301

Johnson County Community
College
Overland Park, KS 66210

Pratt Community College
Pratt, KS 67124

Louisiana

Bossier Parish Community
College
Bossier City, LA 71111

Delgado Community College
New Orleans, LA 70119

Maine

Northern Maine Vocational
Technical Institute
Presque Isle, ME 04769

Maryland

Cecil Community College
North East, MD 21901

Chesapeake College
Wye Mills, MD 21679

Garrett Community College
McHenry, MD 21541

Michigan

Alpena Community College
Alpena, MI 49707

Charles Stewart Mott
Community College
Flint, MI 48503

Delta College
University Center, MI 48710

Macomb County Community
College
Warren, MI 48093

Mid Michigan Community
College
Harrison, MI 48625

Northwestern Michigan
College
Traverse City, MI 49684

Oakland Community College
Bloomfield Hills, MI 48013

Schoolcraft College
Livonia, MI 48152

West Shore Community
College
Scottville, MI 49454

Minnesota

University of Minnesota
Technical
College–Crookston
Crookston, MN 56716

University of Minnesota
Technical College–Waseca
Waseca, MN 56093

Worthington Community
College
Worthington, MN 56187

Mississippi

Coahoama Junior College
Clarksdale, MS 38614

Copiah-Lincoln Junior College
Wesson, MS 39191

East Central Junior College
Decatur, MS 39327

Holmes Junior College
Goodman, MS 39079

Itawamba Community College
Fulton, MS 38843

Meridian Community College
Meridian, MS 39301

Mississippi Delta Junior
College
Moorhead, MS 38761

Mississippi Gulf Coast
Community College
Perkinston, MS 39573

Missouri

Crowder College
Neosho, MO 64850

East Central College
Union, MO 63084

Moberly Area Junior College
Moberly, MO 65270

State Fair Community College
Sedalia, MO 65301

Montana

Dawson Community College
Glendrive, MT 59330

Flathead Valley Community
College
Kalispell, MT 59901

Nebraska

Central Community College,
Platte Campus
Columbus, NE 68601

Mid-Plains Community
College
North Platte, NE 69101

Northeast Community College
Norfolk, NE 68701

Western Nebraska Community
College
Sidney, NE 69162

Nevada

Clark County Community
College
North Las Vegas, NV 89030

Truckee Meadows Community
College
Reno, NV 89512

Western Nevada Community
College
Carson City, NV 89701

New Hampshire

New Hampshire
Vocational-Technical
College
Manchester, NH 03102

New Jersey

Middlesex County College
Edison, NJ 08818

Passaic County Community
College
Paterson, NJ 07509

New Mexico

Eastern New Mexico
University—Clovis
Clovis, NM 88101

Eastern New Mexico
University—Roswell
Roswell, NM 88202

New Mexico Junior College
Hobbs, NM 88240

Northern New Mexico
Community College
El Rito, NM 87530

New York

Dutchess Community College
Poughkeepsie, NY 12601

Mohawk Valley Community
College
Utica, NY 13501

State University of New York
College of Agriculture
and Technology at
Morrisville
Morrisville, NY 13408

State University of New York
College of Technology at
Delhi
Delhi, NY 13617

North Carolina

Anson Community College
Ansonville, NC 28007

Ashville Buncombe Technical
College
Ashville, NC 28801

Beaufort County Community
College
Washington, NC 27889

Catawba Valley Community
College
Hickory, NC 28601

Central Piedmont Community
College
Charlotte, NC 28235

Coastal Carolina Community
College
Jacksonville, NC 28540

Forsyth Technical Community
College
Winston-Salem, NC 27103

Isothermal Community College
Spindale, NC 28160

Mitchell Community College
Statesville, NC 28677

Rockingham Community
  College
  Wentworth, NC 27375

Southeastern Community
  College
  Whiteville, NC 28472

Tri-County Community
  College
  Murphy, NC 28906

Wilkes Community College
  Wilkesboro, NC 28697

North Dakota

Bismarck State College
  Bismarck, ND 58501

North Dakota State College of
  Science
  Wahpeton, ND 58075

Turtle Mountain Community
  College
  Balcourt, ND 58316

University of North
  Dakota–Williston
  Williston, ND 58801

Ohio

Belmont Technical College
  St. Clairsville, OH 43950

Columbus State Community
  College
  Columbus, OH 43216

Lakeland Community College
  Mentor, OH 44060

Terra Technical College
  Fremont, OH 43420

Washington Technical College
  Marietta, OH 45750

Oklahoma

Eastern Oklahoma State
  College
  Wilburton, OK 74578

Murray State College
  Tishomingom, OK 73460

Northeastern Oklahoma
  Agricultural and
  Mechanical College
  Miami, OK 74354

Northern Oklahoma College
  Tonkawa, OK 74653

Tulsa Junior College
  Tulsa, OK 74119

Oregon

Blue Mountain Community
  College
  Pendleton, OR 97801

Central Oregon Community
    College
    Bend, OR 97701

Clatsop Community College
    Astoria, OR 97103

Lane Community College
    Eugene, OR 97405

Linn-Benton Community
    College
    Albany, OR 97321

Mount Hood Community
    College
    Gresham, OR 97030

Portland Community College
    Portland, OR 97219

Rouge Community College
    Grants Pass, OR 97526

Treasure Valley Community
    College
    Ontario, OR 97914

Ompqua Community College
    Roseburg, OR 97470

Pennsylvania

Community College at
    Allegheny County–Boyce
    Monroeville, PA 15146

Community College of
    Allegheny County–North
    Pittsburgh, PA 15237

Community College of
    Allegheny County–South
    West Mifflin, PA 15122

Community College of Beaver
    County
    Monaca, PA 15061

Westmoreland County
    Community College
    Youngwood, PA 15697

South Carolina

Aiken Technical College
    Aiken, SC 29801

Chesterfield-Marlboro
    Technical College
    Cheraw, SC 29520

Denmark Technical College
    Denmark, SC 29042

Florence Darlington Technical
    College
    Florence, SC 29501

Greenville Technical College
    Greenville, SC 29606

Horry-Georgetown Technical
    College
    Conway, SC 29526

Orangeburg-Calhoun Technical
    College
    Orangeburg, SC 29115

Piedmont Technical College
  Greenwood, SC 29646

Spartanburg Technical College
  Spartanburg, SC 29303

Sumter Area Technical College
  Sumter, SC 29150

Tri-County Technical College
  Pendleton, SC 29670

Trident Technical College
  Charleston, SC 29411

York Technical College
  Rock Hill, SC 29730

Tennessee

Chattanooga State Technical
    Community College
  Chattanooga, TN 37406

Cleveland State Community
    College
  Cleveland, TN 37320

State Technical Institute at
    Memphis
  Memphis, TN 38134

Tri-Cities State Technical
    Institute
  Blountville, TN 37616

Texas

Austin Community College
  Austin, TX 78768

Bee County College
  Beeville, TX 78102

Central Texas College
  Killeen, TX 76541

Cisco Junior College
  Cisco, TX 76437

El Paso Community College
  El Paso, TX 79998

Laredo Junior College
  Laredo, TX 78040

Lee College
  Baytown, TX 77520

Midland College
  Midland, TX 79701

Navarro College
  Corsicana, TX 75110

Odessa College
  Odessa, TX 79762

Paris Junior College
  Paris, TX 75460

Ranger Junior College
  Ranger, TX 76470

South Plains College
  Levelland, TX 79336

Southwest Texas Junior College
  Uvalde, TX 78801

Tarrant County Junior College
  Fort Worth, TX 76102

Texarcana College
Texarcana, TX 75501

Wharton County Junior College
Wharton, TX 77488

Utah

College of Eastern Utah
Price, UT 84501

Dixie College
Saint George, UT 84770

Salt Lake Community College
Salt Lake City, UT 84130

Snow College
Ephraim, UT 84627

Utah Valley Community
College
Orem, UT 84058

Virginia

Central Virginia Community
College
Lynchburg, VA 24502

Dabney S. Lancaster
Community College
Clifton Forge, VA 24422

John Tyler Community College
Chester, VA 23831

Mountain Empire Community
College
Big Stone Gap, VA 24219

New River Community College
Dublin, VA 24084

Northern Virginia Community
College
Annandale, VA 22003

Patrick Henry Community
College
Martinsville, VA 24112

Southside Virginia
Community College
Alberta, VA 23821

Southwest Virginia
Community College
Richlands, VA 24641

Thomas Nelson Community
College
Hampton, VA 23670

Tidewater Community College
Portsmouth, VA 23703

Virginia Western Community
College
Roanoke, VA 24015

Washington

Big Bend Community College
Moses Lake, WA 98837

Centralia College
Centralia, WA 98531

Clark Community College
Vancouver, WA 98663

Columbia Basin Community
  College
Pasco, WA 99301

Green River Community
  College
Auburn, WA 98002

Olympic College
Bremerton, WA 98310

Shoreline Community College
Seattle, WA 98133

Spokane Community College
Spokane, WA 99207

Walla Walla Community
  College
Walla Walla, WA 99362

West Virginia

Parkersburg Community
  College
Parkersburg, WV 26101

Southern West Virginia
  Community College
Logan, WV 25601

Wisconsin

Fox Valley Technical College
Appleton, WI 54913

Lakeshore Technical College
Cleveland, WI 53015

Madison Area Technical
  College
Madison, WI 53703

Milwaukee Area Technical
  College
Milwaukee, WI 53203

Wyoming

Central Wyoming College
Riverton, WY 82501

Eastern Wyoming College
Torrington, WY 82240

VGM CAREER BOOKS

OPPORTUNITIES IN
Available in both paperback and hardbound editions

Accounting Careers
Acting Careers
Advertising Careers
Aerospace Careers
Agriculture Careers
Airline Careers
Animal and Pet Care
Appraising Valuation Science
Architecture
Automotive Service
Banking
Beauty Culture
Biological Sciences
Biotechnology Careers
Book Publishing Careers
Broadcasting Careers
Building Construction Trades
Business Communication Careers
Business Management
Cable Television
Carpentry Careers
Chemical Engineering
Chemistry Careers
Child Care Careers
Chiropractic Health Care
Civil Engineering Careers
Commercial Art and Graphic Design
Computer Aided Design and Computer Aided Mfg.
Computer Maintenance Careers
Computer Science Careers
Counseling & Development
Crafts Careers
Culinary Careers
Dance
Data Processing Careers
Dental Care
Drafting Careers
Electrical Trades
Electronic and Electrical Engineering
Energy Careers
Engineering Careers
Engineering Technology Careers
Environmental Careers
Eye Care Careers
Fashion Careers
Fast Food Careers
Federal Government Careers
Film Careers
Financial Careers
Fire Protection Services
Fitness Careers
Food Services
Foreign Language Careers
Forestry Careers
Gerontology Careers
Government Service
Graphic Communications
Health and Medical Careers
High Tech Careers
Home Economics Careers
Hospital Administration
Hotel & Motel Management
Human Resources Management Careers
Industrial Design
Information Systems Careers
Insurance Careers
Interior Design

International Business
Journalism Careers
Landscape Architecture
Laser Technology
Law Careers
Law Enforcement and Criminal Justice
Library and Information Science
Machine Trades
Magazine Publishing Careers
Management
Marine & Maritime Careers
Marketing Careers
Materials Science
Mechanical Engineering
Medical Technology Careers
Microelectronics
Military Careers
Modeling Careers
Music Careers
Newspaper Publishing Careers
Nursing Careers
Nutrition Careers
Occupational Therapy Careers
Office Occupations
Opticianry
Optometry
Packaging Science
Paralegal Careers
Paramedical Careers
Part-time & Summer Jobs
Performing Arts Careers
Petroleum Careers
Pharmacy Careers
Photography
Physical Therapy Careers
Physician Careers
Plumbing & Pipe Fitting
Podiatric Medicine
Printing Careers
Property Management Careers
Psychiatry
Psychology
Public Health Careers
Public Relations Careers
Purchasing Careers
Real Estate
Recreation and Leisure
Refrigeration and Air Conditioning Trades
Religious Service
Restaurant Careers
Retailing
Robotics Careers
Sales Careers
Sales & Marketing
Secretarial Careers
Securities Industry
Social Science Careers
Social Work Careers
Speech-Language Pathology Careers
Sports & Athletics
Sports Medicine
State and Local Government
Teaching Careers
Technical Communications
Telecommunications
Television and Video Careers
Theatrical Design & Production
Transportation Careers

Travel Careers
Veterinary Medicine Careers
Vocational and Technical Careers
Welding Careers
Word Processing
Writing Careers
Your Own Service Business

CAREERS IN
Accounting
Advertising
Business
Communications
Computers
Education
Engineering
Health Care
Science

CAREER DIRECTORIES
Careers Encyclopedia
Occupational Outlook Handbook

CAREER PLANNING
Admissions Guide to Selective Business Schools
Career Planning and Development for College Students
  and Recent Graduates
Careers Checklists
Careers for Bookworms and Other Literary Types
Careers for Sports Nuts
Handbook of Business and Management Careers
Handbook of Scientific and Technical Careers
How to Change Your Career
How to Get and Get Ahead On Your First Job
How to Get People to Do Things Your Way
How to Have a Winning Job Interview
How to Land a Better Job
How to Make the Right Career Moves
How to Prepare for College
How to Run Your Own Home Business
How to Write a Winning Résumé
Joyce Lain Kennedy's Career Book
Life Plan
Planning Your Career of Tomorrow
Planning Your College Education
Planning Your Military Career
Planning Your Young Child's Education

SURVIVAL GUIDES
Dropping Out or Hanging In
High School Survival Guide
College Survival Guide

VGM Career Horizons
a division of *NTC Publishing Group*
4255 West Touhy Avenue
Lincolnwood, Illinois 60646-1975 U.S.A.